C000144971

LITTLE BOOK OF
SCOTLAND

LITTLE BOOK OF
SCOTLAND

First published in the UK in 2013

© Demand Media Limited 2013

www.demand-media.co.uk

Printed and bound in China

ISBN 978-1-909217-30-0

Contents

Introduction

Sitting at the northernmost extremity of the British Isles, brooding over the vast expanse of the Atlantic Ocean and the chilly waters of the North Sea, Scotland is among the planet's most captivating lands. Boasting soaring mountain peaks and rocky glens, rushing rivers and peaceful lowlands, as well as nearly eight hundred islands clustering round its shores, this is a country that is also fiercely proud of the industrial and scientific heritage that is celebrated in its major cities.

Each year, millions of visitors also revel in Scotland's unique culture, warm to her welcoming people and marvel at her fascinating history. There are ancient castles and mysterious lochs to be explored, rocky coasts to be wondered

at, a thousand outdoor activities to be shared, festivals and sporting events to be experienced, magnificent wildlife to be watched. Scotland is a country one could never tire of.

What is Scotland? The reference books will tell you it's part of the United Kingdom (although perhaps for not much longer) with many powers of self-government thanks to the UK's policy of devolution. Its lands cover nearly eighty thousand square kilometres (about the same size as the Czech Republic), with nearly two per cent of that total accounted for by the water of its lochs and rivers. Its population is around 5.3 million and on average there are sixty-eight people for every square kilometre of land – many less

than the UK average of 256 per square kilometre. Scotland is a country that is largely and noticeably empty of the human species.

Its highest point is the famed mountain of Ben Nevis in Lochaber, which reaches skywards for 1,344 metres. Its longest river is the Tay, whose waters empty into the North Sea after a journey of 190 kilometres. If you wanted to discover the geographical centre of Scotland, you would find yourself a few miles from the village of Newtonmore in the Highlands.

Scotland's variety of landscapes have been greatly influenced by the movements of huge glaciers that covered its surface in the Pleistocene ice ages, between about 2.5 million and 11,700 years ago. To the north of the Highland Boundary Fault, which traverses the country from Arran to Stonehaven, lie the Highlands and Islands, where the geography and geology are markedly different from those of the area below the fault line. In the north the land is rocky and mountainous, containing the UK's loftiest peaks in massifs like the Cairngorms and the Cuillins of Skye, and you are never far from one of the lochs that dot the map. Some coasts consist of machair, a low-lying dune pastureland. Beyond the coasts lie the hundreds of islands, most of which can be divided into four groups: the Inner Hebrides, the Outer Hebrides, Orkney and Shetland.

Below the Highland Boundary Fault lie the Central Lowlands, a rift valley

bearing the iron and coal that fuelled the nation's Industrial Revolution. This is an area that once witnessed much volcanic activity; one of Scotland's most familiar sights, Arthur's Seat in Edinburgh, is what remains of what was once a much larger volcano. Mostly low-lying, the Central Lowlands nevertheless have their own high points, among which are the Campsie Fells and the Ochil Hills.

If you continue further south you will enter the Southern Uplands, which lie below another fault line running from Girvan in the west to Dunbar in the east. This region consists of a range of hills some two hundred kilometres in length, between which run broad valleys. Here you will find the highest village in the UK: Wanlockhead, 430 metres above sea level.

Scotland's border with its southern neighbour England runs for ninety-six kilometres between the Solway Firth in the west and the basin of the River Tweed in the east. As we'll see, it is a border whose establishment was fought over for many centuries. To find the country's other nearest neighbours, you will need to travel westwards to Ireland (thirty kilometres away from the Kintyre peninsula), north to the Faroe Islands (nearly three hundred kilometres) and eastwards more than three hundred kilometres from Aberdeenshire to Norway.

What kind of weather can the visitor to Scotland expect? The kind that can change from one minute to the next is the short answer. In general, however, the country enjoys a temperate climate given its northerly latitude – it's usually much warmer than similarly located places like southern Scandinavia and Labrador.

That's because of the influence of the Gulf Stream, the Atlantic current whose warm waters bathe the west coast and its islands. It's these regions that generally enjoy the warmest weather Scotland has to offer, but also the wettest.

Scotland has long been an economic powerhouse, and it continues to punch above its weight: it generates nearly ten per cent of the UK's money, despite only containing 8.4 per cent of its population. The economy was for centuries based on heavy manufacturing, with coalmining, shipbuilding and steel production playing starring roles, but now the focus is more on the service industries and the oil that lies under Scottish waters in the North Sea. Tourism, too, is an important contributor to the economy.

In the preceding paragraphs you have read what amounts to little more than a snapshot of Scotland; a taster for what lies ahead in the following chapters.

First we will examine how the Scots came to inhabit their beautiful country, how they struggled for many centuries to establish sovereignty over it and how that sovereignty might one day be restored. We'll take a look at the natural and man-made wonders of the country, how its culture has grown up over the centuries and how it influences the Scotland of today. In one chapter we will discover how great Scottish men and women have changed the world; in others we'll come face to face with the animals that typify the country and the plant life that helps to make it so attractive. Finally, we'll point to a few of the sights you must not miss and have fun with little-known facts about the wonderful country in question.

Welcome to Scotland. Fàilte gu Alba.

Story of the Scots

Scotland has been a long time in the making. The entire country was covered by ice at various stages during the 2.4 million-year period known as the Ice Age – a period that helped to form the glorious landscapes we see today. The movement of vast glaciers, and the meltwater rivers that resulted when they thawed, carved Scotland's hills and valleys. It was only after the final retreat of the great ice sheets, between 15,000 and 12,000 years ago, that early man could start to inhabit Scotland.

Hunter-gatherers began to move into Scotland, and flint artefacts in the region of 12,000 years old have been found in what is now Lanarkshire, but the first signs of settled habitation, dated to 8,500 years ago, have been discovered in Cramond, near Edinburgh. Although there is evidence of domesticity, these early Scots seem to have been highly mobile people who may have moved from site to site as the seasons changed. They used boats for transport and fishing, and also moved well inland to hunt using stone weapons.

As time went on through the Neolithic age, these people began to settle down into farming communities, clearing forests for crops and keeping domestic animals. A large timber-framed building at Balbridie in Aberdeenshire dates back to 3600BC. An equally impressive building with a different purpose is a stone-built, chambered tomb discovered at Maeshowe on Orkney; a carefully aligned entrance

Above: *The Battle of Culloden, 1746 – the last battle fought on British soil*

passageway allowed sunshine to illuminate the main chamber at the winter solstice. A well-preserved stone settlement at Skara Brae on Orkney, dating from 3200BC, shows that covered passageways connected the houses.

With the coming of the Iron Age, in approximately 700BC, the people inhabiting Scotland started to trade and use new technologies. These were Celtic people who took the decoration of metalwork to extraordinarily beautiful lengths, wore colourful clothes and jewellery and produced remarkably intricate knot patterns on stone and other materials. Soon the Roman Empire began to stretch towards Britain, and the Romans came to call the Celtic tribes in the north Caledoni, and their land Caledonia.

The Romans named one of the tribes, who painted or tattooed their bodies, the Picts (the 'painted people'). The Picts are perpetuated in the names of towns deriving from their language, such as Urquhart (by the thicket) and Aberdeen (mouth of the Don). After the Roman conquest of Britain, the tribes of Caledonia fought hard to keep the invaders out of their territory; for their part, the Romans were keen to keep the tribes out of the south. In efforts to keep the peace they built two mighty fortifications: Hadrian's Wall, which was begun in 122AD and extended from Wallsend in the east to the Solway Firth in the west; and the Antonine Wall, which stretched between

Above: *Prince Charles Edward Louis John Casimir Sylvester Severino Maria Stuart – otherwise, and more simply, known as Bonnie Prince Charlie*

Britain by around 410AD, although they had left what is now Scotland to its own devices a couple of centuries earlier. But as one threat to the tribes receded, another hove into view.

The fifth century saw north-western areas of Scotland being raided and settled by Gaels, who were crossing the sea from the north of Ireland in growing numbers. The Gaels, or Scoti, went on to establish the Kingdom of Dalriada in the western parts of Scotland. At about the same time, Angles from the south were busy conquering regions south of the Antonine Wall, which would become the Anglo-Saxon kingdom of Bernicia and even later part of the English kingdom of Northumbria.

It was during the seventh century that Christianity came to Scotland in the form of the Irish missionary Columba, who founded a monastery on the Hebridean isle of Iona and introduced the Scoti to Celtic Christianity. He met with less success when it came to converting the Picts, who were in any case wary of anything that would bring them closer to the Scoti.

In common with many areas of the British Isles and other parts of Europe, Scotland came to the attention of seafaring

the Firth of Forth and the Firth of Clyde. The latter, completed around 155AD, marked the northern extremity of the Roman Empire.

All empires eventually crumble, and the Roman Empire was no exception. The Romans had finally abandoned

gangs of Vikings from the eighth century onwards, and eventually all of Scotland's kingdoms had been overthrown to some extent by the men in the longships. Out of adversity came something positive, however: the warring Pict and Scoti tribes ended their age-old hostility towards each other and, in the ninth century, banded together to form the Kingdom of Scotland. Whether the union of the groups came about through a Pictish takeover of Dalriada or the other way about is debated by historians. Whichever way it happened, the date traditionally

the Catholic Church, Constantine II, reigned for an extraordinary forty-two years.

The reign of a later king, Duncan I (1034-1040) was marked by a number of unsuccessful military ventures, and it was ended by a name familiar throughout the world: MacBeth. He was overthrown by another well-known name: Malcolm III, known as the Great Chief (Cenn Mór). Malcolm ushered in the era of the Dunkeld dynasty, a family line that ruled Scotland for the following two centuries. However, Malcolm III had submitted to the invading William the Conqueror, thus leaving the Scottish throne open to English claims.

The throne changed hands several times, and by the twelfth century Anglo-Norman barons, including the Bruce family, were laying claim to much of Scotland. In exchange for land, the barons helped King David I (himself an English baron) to further his claim to the throne and introduce the feudal system of land tenure to large parts of Scotland. Members of the Anglo-Norman aristocracy came to prominence and the first royal burghs were founded.

In the thirteenth century, Alexander II and his son Alexander III pursued a

given to this momentous event is 843.

The first king of this united kingdom was Kenneth MacAlpin who, together with his descendants, formed the royal House of Alpin. This was no peaceful dynasty, for successions to the throne were frequently disputed. At the death of Donald II in 900, he was described as King of Alba – the first king to be so named. The king often credited with bringing Scottish Christianity into alignment with policy of peace with England in order to strengthen their bid to make the Norwegian territories in the west of Scotland their own. The Norwegian king Haakon Haakonarson sent a massive fleet in an attempt to hold on to his possessions, and in September 1263 Alexander III's and Haakon's forces met at the Battle of Largs in Ayrshire. Stalemate was the end result. But in 1266, with the Treaty of Perth, Norway surrendered Scotland's western seaboard to Alexander.

There was still much dispute and blood to be spilt over the sovereignty of Scotland, which was still to win its freedom from England. The throne passed through the hands of the houses of Balliol and Bruce in the following years, and in 1295 King John entered into an alliance with France, known ever after as the Auld Alliance. English invasion, under the leadership of Edward I, followed. Scottish landowner Sir William Wallace came to the fore as a military leader and defeated an English army at the Battle of Stirling Bridge in 1297.

Wallace served as Guardian of Scotland until his defeat at the Battle of Falkirk the following year. He initially escaped the clutches of the English but was captured near Glasgow in 1305 and handed over

to Edward. The rest will be familiar to those who have watched the otherwise historically dubious film *Braveheart*. Wallace was hanged, drawn and quartered for high treason, despite the fact that he owed no allegiance to England.

Robert Bruce was appointed joint Guardian with John Comyn in Wallace's place, and was promoted to King in 1306, soon after having participated in Comyn's murder. Bruce inflicted a significant defeat on the English under Edward II at the Battle of Bannockburn in 1314, securing a kind of independence in the process.

Soon after, an intervention by the Pope allowed Scotland's sovereignty to be recognised by the major dynasties of Europe. The year 1326 saw what was perhaps the first full session of the Parliament of Scotland, and two years later Edward III signed the treaty of Northampton, acknowledging independence under the rule of Robert the Bruce.

But it wasn't long – four years, to be exact – before the English invaded again, giving rise to the Second War of Independence. Their efforts to install Edward Balliol on the Scottish throne failed, however, and in 1371 the first of the Stuart (or Stewart) kings, Robert II, came to power. Nine Stuart monarchs were to rule Scotland before 1603, when further powers were to come the dynasty's way.

During the reigns of those kings, much of great importance occurred in Scotland that served to help form the country we know today. In 1468, for example, James III married Margaret of Denmark, receiving the Orkney Islands and the Shetland Islands by way of a dowry. While Berwick-upon-Tweed was lost to the English in 1482, further territory came the way of Scotland six years later when James IV ended the semi-independent rule of the Lord of the Isles to bring the Western Isles under the monarch's rule for the first time. An indicator of future events came in 1503, when the same James married Margaret Tudor, the daughter of Henry VII of England.

The reign of James IV witnessed a great flowering of Scottish culture as the influence of the European Renaissance

Above: *Kirriemuir stone – one of a number of Pictish carved stones found in Angus and indicating that Kirriemuir was an important ecclesiastical centre in the first millennium AD*

grew. The fifteenth century also saw significant developments in the field of education with the founding of three universities and the passing of the Education Act, with its decree that the sons of barons and important freeholders should attend grammar schools.

In 1512 the Auld Alliance between Scotland and France was renewed and the following year, when England under Henry VIII attacked the French, James IV

Above: *Pictish silver – part of a hoard found at Norrie's Law, near Largo in Fife*

retaliated with an invasion of England. The result was the disastrous Battle of Flodden Field, at which the king and around ten thousand Scottish troops were killed – a bloody event that is commemorated in the song *Flowers of the Forest*.

Further Stuart sorties against England culminated in the Battle of Solway Moss in 1542 – another defeat for Scotland and, apparently, so hard for James V to take that he died of a broken heart. The day before his death he was told of the birth of a daughter, the girl who would grow up to become Mary, Queen of Scots.

Mary was brought up in Catholic France and married the Dauphin, who became Francis II of that country. When her husband died Mary returned to Scotland to wear the crown. Her reign was notable for the number of crises it endured. They were largely provoked by the Catholic nobles of Scotland, who disapproved of Mary's reluctance to impose her and their religion on the populace.

Married successively to Lord Darnley (who was murdered) and the Earl of Bothwell (who was implicated in the murder), she was eventually taken and imprisoned by Bothwell's rivals. Languishing in Loch Leven Castle, Mary was forced to abdicate in 1567, and the crown passed to her infant son, who became James VI. While the intrigues continued, Mary escaped and fled to England, where she became the focal point for Catholic conspirators. Her days were numbered. Tried for treason on the orders of Elizabeth I, Mary was executed in 1587.

Meanwhile, Scotland had been undergoing a religious revolution under the influence of Calvinism. The country's Parliament had in 1560 adopted a confession of faith that rejected the Mass and the jurisdiction of the Pope. In

England, Henry VIII had separated the Church of England from Rome in 1534.

In 1603, following the death of Elizabeth I without an heir, James VI of Scotland acceded to the English throne, thus also becoming James I of England. The crowns of the two countries remained separate, despite James's efforts to create a throne of Great Britain. The acquisition of Irish sovereignty allowed Protestant Scots to settle in the province of Ulster, reversing the movement of centuries before that had created the Kingdom of Dalriada.

There followed a period of great unrest and bloodshed throughout Scotland. It was not until 1660, after the English Civil War, the Commonwealth of Oliver Cromwell and the restoration of Charles II to the throne that Scotland became once again an independent kingdom. Under James VII (James II of England), the last Catholic to reign in Britain, Protestant subjects were alienated, and William of Orange was invited by leading Englishmen to land with an army and claim the throne. James fled, in what became known as the Glorious Revolution.

James's supporters (Jacobites) could not accept the status quo and there followed a series of risings against the crown. The

Left: *'True Picture of a women (sic) Picte' – engraving by Theodor de Bry, 1590*

revolution was decisively put down at the Battle of Dunkeld in 1689, but there was more to come. Thirty-eight members of the Clan MacDonald were massacred in Glencoe, in the Highlands, by the Earl of Argyll's Regiment of Foot because they had not pledged allegiance to William and his wife Mary (the daughter of James VII) quickly enough.

Finally, the kingdoms of Scotland and England were united politically and economically by the Acts of Union of

1707. With Wales, the countries now formed the new nation of Great Britain.

The Jacobite cause, however, continued to play a major role in the affairs of the new state. Jacobites found the union unacceptable, and their efforts to wrest control of the throne from the Hanoverian dynasty culminated in the military campaigns of Charles Edward Stuart, better known as Bonnie Prince Charlie or the Young Pretender. With the support of several clans he took Edinburgh and Carlisle and marched as far south as Derby before retreating to Scotland. Pursued further and further north by the Duke of Cumberland – known as the Butcher – Charles and his army were finally routed at the Battle of Culloden, east of Inverness, in 1746. The Jacobites had finally been crushed, with Charles managing to escape to France.

The eighteenth century in Scotland saw the beginning of a great outpouring of Scottish intellectual and scientific genius. The Enlightenment then in full flower in Europe flourished likewise in Scotland, and there were huge advancements in the arts, philosophy, economics, medicine, architecture, law, agriculture and many other fields of human accomplishment. By 1750, Scotland could boast a literacy level of around seventy-five per cent, making its citizens some of Europe's most literate people, and this was the time when names such as Robert Burns (writer), Adam Smith (economist), Joseph Black (physicist and chemist) and James Hutton (the first modern geologist) came to the fore. There were many others.

The Union with England and Wales also brought Scotland massive economic and commercial benefits, and the coming Industrial Revolution helped to transform the country from the poor agricultural society it had been in 1750 into one of Europe's leading industrial powerhouses. In the years following 1815 Glasgow, in particular, emerged as a major centre for the textile, iron, coal, leather, sugar, soap and glass industries, among others. Important banks had already been established in Edinburgh in the seventeenth and eighteenth centuries, and Glasgow followed as Scotland became the centre of a flourishing financial system.

The country's population grew rapidly in the nineteenth century, from 1.6 million in 1801 to 4.5 million in 1901. Alongside the explosion in population came a blooming of Scotland's industrial powers as it became a world force in shipbuilding, engineering and locomotive

and railway construction, helped by its many entrepreneurs and engineers and ready supplies of easily mined coal.

By 1900, Scotland's four most industrialised counties – Lanarkshire, Renfrewshire, Dunbartonshire and Ayrshire – held forty-four per cent of the country's population and Glasgow, one of the world's largest cities, was known as the Second City of the Empire after London. By the time World War I broke out in 1914, Scotland was able to send 690,000 men to fight. Losses were disastrously heavy, however: 74,000

Above: *North Sea oil rig – major component of today's Scottish economy*

Far Left: *Shipbuilding on the River Clyde, Glasgow – contributed enormously to Scotland's reputation for quality engineering and manufacture*

Right: *Skara Brae – Neolithic settlement on Orkney serves as a reminder of Scotland's past*

men died in combat or from disease and 150,000 were grievously wounded. Scots comprised just ten per cent of the British population; they made up fifteen per cent of the armed forces; yet they accounted for twenty per cent of the dead.

Worldwide economic depression followed the war, and it hit Scotland particularly hard. Unemployment was high, political agitation widespread, and the Government was fearful of an uprising, at one point deploying tanks and troops in the centre of Glasgow. Resistance had turned to passive despair by the end of the 1920s but, with all the main political parties committed to the Union, new groupings began to emerge. The Scottish National Party (SNP) was formed in 1934 with the express aim of recreating an independent Scotland.

Following World War II, the country's economic and social fortunes took another nosedive as overseas competition and industrial unrest took their toll. But a corner was turned in the 1970s with the exploitation of gas and oil in the North Sea and the turning of the economy away from heavy industry and towards the service sector. There were renewed calls for Scottish independence, or at least devolution of powers from London to Edinburgh, but a referendum on devolution in 1979 proved unsuccessful for the nationalists. Nevertheless, the SNP was by now a significant force in British politics.

When the Labour Party – led by two politicians with Scottish sympathies, Tony Blair and Gordon Brown – was returned to

power in 1997, the way became clear for change. A further referendum confirmed that the Scottish people wanted devolved powers, and the Scottish Parliament duly opened for business in 1999.

Now, with the SNP in the driving seat in the Holyrood parliament building, all eyes are on the Scottish people as they prepare to vote on the question: should Scotland be an independent country? More than four hundred years after the historic Acts of Union, Scotland could soon once again be an independent nation.

Banks and Braes

Scotland can rival any country for beauty, but what sets it apart from almost anywhere on the planet is the extraordinary variety of its landscapes. Mountain and moorland sit cheek by jowl with gently undulating lowlands and dense forests; spectacular rocky coasts lead to the wildernesses and mystery of the isles; bustling towns and cities and great centres of industry have peaceful villages lying in their shadows. It's unlikely you'll find such a fulfilling diversity of things to see, do and wonder at anywhere on Earth.

The wonders start as soon as you reach Scotland. If you're driving north to enter the country on the west, you'll find yourself in the region of Dumfries and Galloway, an area as rich in history as it is in natural loveliness.

One of the first sights to take in is the Old Blacksmith's Shop in Gretna Green, scene of many a runaway wedding in days gone by and still the venue for thousands of marriages. Runaway couples took advantage of Scotland's more relaxed marriage laws here from 1712 – a declaration before two witnesses sufficed, and anybody was permitted to conduct the ceremony. The blacksmiths in Gretna became known as anvil priests.

Dumfries and Galloway is a region of green forests, rolling landscapes and sandy beaches, and it's also home to the 'Queen of the South', the town of Dumfries. The region's strong connections with

the national bard, Robert Burns, can be explored here. Eight miles west on the Solway Coast Heritage Trail lies the village of New Abbey, where the historic Sweetheart Abbey may be found. It was founded in 1273 by Lady Dervorgilla, who lies at rest within … next to her husband's embalmed heart.

Further along the Heritage Trail can be found one of Scotland's most remarkable buildings: the triangular Caerlaverock Castle, built in the thirteenth century. At the town of Kirkcudbright you'll find a wealth of art galleries and studios, while if food is more your thing head for Castle Douglas, famed for its market and farming traditions. The Galloway Red Kite Trail around Loch Ken allows you to watch

these beautiful birds while taking in some lovely scenery – and you can explore New Galloway, Scotland's smallest royal burgh, along the way.

Galloway Forest Park, Britain's largest park of its kind, is a great attraction for walkers and mountain bikers, while the town of Newton Stewart, sitting among hills on the River Cree, is famous for its trout and salmon fishing. The Isle of Whithorn is known for its connections with Saint Ninian, an early Christian missionary among the Picts.

The Rhinns peninsula – an area with a spectacular coastline, many small bays and a varied landscape – stretches twenty-five miles to the Mull of Galloway, Scotland's southernmost point. At the north end

Above: *The Old Blacksmith's Shop at Gretna Green – scene of many a runaway wedding in days gone by*

Above: *Floors Castle, Kelso – the seat of the Duke of Roxburghe, built in the 1720s*

of Dumfries and Galloway, nestling among wonderful scenery is the market town of Sanquar, where you may send a postcard from the world's oldest post office. The former lead mining village of Wanlockhead is the highest village in Scotland at 467 metres above sea level.

Over to the east lies the region of the Scottish Borders, home to rolling valleys, extensive forests and magnificent heather moorlands. This is the land that inspired Sir Walter Scott, acclaimed as the inventor of the modern historical novel, to write his tales of adventure such as *Rob Roy* and *Ivanhoe*. It's no surprise the young Scott was so inspired by the folk tales of the region, for over many centuries it bore the brunt of invasions from the south and provided a staging post for armies heading into England.

This was also the land of the Border Reivers, men whose horseback raids served to fill their families' larders and whose sure-footed steeds aided their guerilla tactics in the wars of independence. Nowadays the Reivers' feats and their mounts are remembered in the region's annual Common Riding events. The sense of regional identity is strong in the Borders.

Its towns, including the textile strongholds of Hawick, Selkirk, Galashiels and Peebles, are well worth exploring, and the abbey towns of Jedburgh, Kelso and Melrose contain historic treasures. Kelso, where the young Walter Scott spent his formative years, has an eighteenth century market square that is Scotland's largest. The neighbouring Floors Castle, the country's biggest inhabited castle, is home to the Duke and Duchess of Roxburghe.

The fishing industry is still active in the coastal town of Eyemouth, which sits five miles north of the border. It's a fascinating town with cobbled streets, narrow pends (archways) and wynds (passageways), a natural harbour and sandy beaches. Inland at Selkirk, the local people are known as souters (shoemakers). One Selkirk man, Fletcher, is commemorated by a statue outside Victoria Hall. He is said to have been the only warrior to return from the Scots' terrible defeat at the Battle of Flodden in 1513 – and he died soon after his return.

For a taste of Scottish victory you can view Neidpath Castle near Peebles: here the English were defeated three times in one day. The castle overlooks the River Tweed, which flows 160 kilometres through the Borders before reaching Berwick-upon-Tweed. The river is justly famed for its salmon and trout: it's said that more Atlantic salmon are caught in its waters than in any other European river.

For more history, visit Traquair House, south-east of Peebles, which is reputed to be Scotland's oldest continually inhabited house. Dating from 1107, it was built as a hunting lodge for Scottish kings and queens.

Travelling westwards in our exploration of Scotland, we can gain our first taste of life on a Scottish isle in the region of Ayrshire and Arran. This is also a region of unspoilt coastlines, some of Scotland's best beaches, spectacular rolling hills and leisure activities aplenty including, if you wish, a round of golf at the first course to stage the Open Championship.

Prestwick was not only the scene of that momentous event, it also witnessed the first hole in one – or at least the first

Above: *Summit of Goatfell – highest point on the Isle of Arran*

nineteenth century, but there's been a fortress on the site since the fifth century. An overview of the Isle's history can be found at the Arran Heritage Museum.

That great Scottish hero William Wallace's connections with Ayrshire are remembered in the town of Ayr, where the Wallace Tower stands proudly in the middle of the High Street. Another legendary historical figure, Robert the Bruce, is thought to have been born in Turnberry Castle, the ruins of which can be seen on the coast north of Girvan. The Bruce is said to have ordered the castle's destruction in 1310, to prevent it from falling into English hands.

Tributes to Robert Burns, a local man, can be found all over Ayrshire, and the most important collection of his life and works is to be seen in his birthplace, the village of Alloway south of Ayr. The Robert Burns Birthplace Museum consists of the cottage where he was born, the landmarks where he set his greatest works, a monument and gardens created in his honour and a modern museum.

In a land of castles, one of the most notable is the cliff-top Culzean, near Maybole. Its lovely surroundings and Robert Adam architecture make it one of Scotland's favourite attractions.

to be recorded – by Young Tom Morris in 1868. The Open is also held regularly at the nearby Royal Troon and Turnberry clubs, but golfers looking for less prestigious challenges can choose from a wealth of links, heathland, parkland and moorland courses.

Travellers who wish to explore the distant past need only visit the wonderful Isle of Arran, which has earned the title of Scotland in Miniature. The Bronze Age can be imagined at Machrie Moor, where five stone circles await the visitor after a walk of one and a half miles. Bringing you further up to date, Brodick Castle, set against the backdrop of Goatfell mountain, has a red sandstone aspect dating from the

It's time to turn eastwards, to the region of Edinburgh and the Lothians, and to Scotland's grand capital city itself – the UK's second most popular tourist destination. Edinburgh, world famous for its architecture and contribution to culture, is dominated by its twelfth century castle, perched atop an extinct volcano and home to Scotland's crown jewels, the National War Museum and much else besides. Here, Iron Age warriors defended their hill fort, Scots and English fought during the wars of independence and Mary, Queen of Scots gave birth to King James VI.

A camera obscura on the Royal Mile (a series of streets forming the main thoroughfare of Edinburgh's Old Town), allows the visitor a unique view of this historic city, which has been dubbed Auld Reekie. If you want to find out what life was like in centuries gone by, visit Mary King's Close. This is a warren of underground streets and spaces, dating from the 1600s, which were once open to the skies.

Above: *Edinburgh Castle, seen from Princes Street Gardens – scene of battles and births*

Edinburgh, home every summer to the world's biggest annual arts festival, is also a shoppers' paradise and an important financial and political centre. The old and the new sit side by side at the lower end of the Royal Mile at Holyrood, where the Scottish Parliament building complements the Palace of Holyroodhouse, official home in Scotland of monarchs of the UK. The New Town of Edinburgh, considered a masterpiece of early city planning, was built between 1765 and 1850 and still delights visitors with its neo-classical and Georgian architecture.

Outside the capital, there are many more connections with Mary, Queen of Scots. She is reputed to have played at the Old Golf Course in Musselburgh, one of the world's first courses, and Linlithgow Palace was once her home. The magnificent ruins are set in a picturesque park beside a loch, and nearby is the fifteenth century St Michael's Kirk, where the queen was baptised. Follow the Linlithgow Heritage Trail to discover more about the town's history.

On the southern shore of the Firth of Forth can be seen the formidable outline of Blackness Castle, built in the fifteenth century by the powerful Crichton family. Often called 'the ship that never sailed', the castle served as a garrison fortress, state prison and ammunition depot. Less intimidating is Hopetoun House in South Queensferry, built for the Hope family more than three hundred years ago and still their home.

Drive west from Edinburgh and the Lothians and you will arrive in Glasgow, a very different city from the capital. Home to more than a million souls (Glasgow and its region account for over forty per cent of Scotland's population), this city grew from a small rural settlement on the River Clyde to become one of the largest seaports in the world and a powerhouse of the shipbuilding and marine engineering industries.

Glasgow is far from being just about industry, however. The city welcomes droves of visitors to its museums, galleries and crowded shopping centres, and its architecture is rightly acclaimed. And the Clyde valley offers more than just a glimpse into Scotland's industrial heritage.

The name Glasgow comes from the Gaelic for 'dear green place', and nowhere is that name better earned than at Kelvingrove Park, which follows the course of the River Kelvin and crosses it at several points. It contains a world-famous museum and art galleries and was designed by Sir Joseph Paxton, whose other works included London's Crystal Palace. While we're on the subject of glasshouses, a trip to Glasgow's Botanic Gardens will reveal the ornate Kibble Palace, built in 1873 to house tropical plants from around the world.

The People's Palace, set in Glasgow Green, tells the story of the city and its people through the media of historic artefacts, paintings, prints, photographs, film and interactive computer displays. In the Winter Gardens next door you will find another tropical glasshouse and the home of the World Pipe Band Championships, which attract forty thousand spectators and eight thousand pipers and drummers from around the world.

Glasgow's contribution to the arts world is significant. The world's largest permanent display of the work of James McNeill Whistler can be found at the Hunterian Art Gallery. Here also, within the Mackintosh House, you can inspect meticulously reconstructed interiors from the home of Charles Rennie Mackintosh, influential architect, designer and artist.

South-east of Glasgow, the Falls of Clyde Wildlife Reserve offers a riverside

Above: *Corra Linn, one of the Falls of Clyde near New Lanark – immortalised in verse by William Wordsworth*

walk past waterfalls and the chance to spot otters or some of a hundred bird species. The reserve forms part of the sixty-eight kilometre Clyde Valley Tourist Route, which takes in several historical attractions. North of Glasgow, in Milngavie, can be found the beginning of the West Highland Way, a 150-kilometre long distance path weaving its way up to Fort William.

Right: Falkland Palace, Fife – acquired by the Scottish Crown in the fourteenth century

Back in the East, facing Edinburgh over the Firth of Forth, one of the most important Pictish kingdoms of ancient Scotland has for long been known as the Kingdom of Fife. This is a region steeped in history, and it shows: magnificent castles, historic towns, splendid cathedrals and sites of historic importance abound. In addition, Fife boasts quaint fishing villages, stunning landscapes and a smattering of modern culture among its attractions.

The town of Dunfermline was once Scotland's capital, established by Malcolm III in the eleventh century as a base of royal power. A wonderful example of Romanesque architecture can be found in Dunfermline Palace and Abbey, resting place of kings and queens including Robert the Bruce. The neighbouring Abbot House, the town's oldest surviving building and a survivor of a great fire in 1624, serves as a heritage centre.

More of the Dunfermline area's royal connections can be explored at Falkland Palace, the country residence of Stuart monarchs for two hundred years and a favourite abode of Mary, Queen of Scots. It's set in the conservation village of Falkland and offers a fascinating glimpse

LITTLE BOOK OF **SCOTLAND**

into the past and, among other features, the oldest real tennis court in Britain.

In the Royal Burgh of Culross you may visit a sixteenth century palace that has been refurbished and has a reconstructed garden, to provide an idea of what life was like in the old days. Culross, believed to have been founded by Saint Serf in the sixth century, is a lovely place full of old buildings and cobbled streets, and was formerly a port and the centre of an industry that manufactured 'girdles' – flat iron plates used for baking over an open fire.

But probably the most well known town in Fife is St Andrews – and there's much more to the place than its world-famous links golf course. St Andrews is known as the home of golf, and with good reason: the Open Championship is often held here and it's also the headquarters of the Royal and Ancient Golf Club, founded in 1754 and the legislative authority for the game throughout most of the world. St Andrews is also home to the third oldest university in the English-speaking world, and the past is evoked in its medieval town centre of narrow alleys and cobbled streets. What's more, the town boasts a twelfth century cathedral that was once Scotland's largest church

and dominated religious affairs until the Protestant Reformation in 1560.

There are more golf courses in Perthshire than you can shake a 3-wood at, but if you're of the opinion that the game is merely a good walk spoilt, you'll be glad to know the region offers much more. There are whisky distilleries to explore and their products to savour, leisurely woodland walks to enjoy and many a historic attraction to discover.

If the more strenuous activity of Munro bagging – the practice of climbing every one of Scotland's Munros, the name

Above: *St Andrews Town Hall – in the home of golf and the location of the English-speaking world's third oldest university*

Right: *The Birnam Oak – familiar to those who know William Shakespeare's Scottish play*

given to mountains over three thousand feet – is your bag, you'll be at home here. Schiehallion (translated as 'fairy hill of the Caledonians'), at over a thousand metres high, is one of Scotland's best-known landmarks, and the Lawers massif contains seven Munros in Perthshire that are linked by a twisting, twenty-five kilometre ridge. Ben Chonzie is the highest point in a vast area of wild land between Loch Tay and Strathearn.

Further down to earth, the Birnam Oak and its neighbour the Birnam Sycamore – mentioned as part of Birnam Wood in Shakespeare's *Macbeth* – are thought to be the only surviving trees of a great forest that once adorned the banks and hillsides of the River Tay. Further woody delights can be found in the town of Crieff, which sits on a tree-covered hill known as the Knock of Crieff.

If you want history in Perthshire, look no further than Scone Palace at the town of the same name (pronounced Skoon). This nineteenth century red sandstone edifice, built by the recasting of a sixteenth century palace, is located on the site of an earlier abbey that was the crowning place of Scottish kings like Macbeth, Robert the Bruce and Charles II. Coronations took place on the Stone of Scone which, after centuries in Westminster, was returned to Scotland in 1996. Also close to Perth is the fascinating Huntingtower Castle, which consists of two towers built in the fifteenth and sixteenth centuries and joined by a range in the seventeenth.

Before visiting the equally intriguing Scottish Crannog Centre near Aberfeldy, you should know that a crannog was a type of loch dwelling of about 2,500 years ago, built on water as a defensive homestead and as a symbol of power and wealth. The centre features a thatched roundhouse in the shallows of Loch Tay that serves as an interactive centre, in which it's possible to find out how life was carried on in the Iron Age.

To the west of Perthshire lies the region of Loch Lomond, the Trossachs and the Forth Valley. As its name suggests, this is a land of shining lochs, snow-capped mountains and dark forests, and it has entranced visitors ever since man set foot in the area.

The Loch Lomond and The Trossachs National Park, Scotland's first national park, consists of nearly two thousand square kilometres of wonderful mountain, glen and loch scenery. Among its delights

are twenty-one Munros, nineteen Corbetts (peaks between 2,500 and 3,000 feet high) and twenty-two large lochs. The park divides into four parts: Loch Lomond, the Trossachs, Breadalbane and Argyll Forest.

Loch Lomond is the largest expanse of fresh water in mainland Britain, measuring up at thirty-nine kilometres long by eight kilometres at its widest point and reaching 190 metres at its deepest. To the north loom mountains while handsome villages line its western shores and a few islands can be found at its south end. The dense forests of the

Above: *Loch Tay – popular freshwater loch for a spot of salmon fishing*

Above: *Falls of Dochart – cascade around the island of Inchbuie, traditional burial place of the MacNab clan*

is said to resemble a shoemaker bending over his last.

If you've had your fill of the great outdoors for a while, this region has plenty of other attractions to offer – indeed, Stirling Castle is one of the most visited locations in Scotland. Sitting on top of a rocky crag, the castle has witnessed many a historic event, including the coronation of Mary, Queen of Scots. The great knight William Wallace is commemorated by the Wallace Monument, just outside the city of Stirling.

Fans of the supernatural will find much to intrigue them at the village of Aberfoyle. In the seventeenth century a certain Reverend Robert Kirk believed the local Doon's Hill was a gateway to the land of the fairies, or 'Secret Commonwealth'. It didn't end well for the Reverend. A pine tree at the hill's summit is said to contain his spirit, imprisoned there by angry fairies.

Study the outline of the region of Argyll and the Isles and you will get an idea of the marvels that await you. Set on Scotland's rugged west coast, this is a fabulous region of sparkling sea lochs, islands, hills and glens, offering more than five thousand kilometres of coastline,

Trossachs are where the outlaw and folk hero Rob Roy, immortalised by Sir Walter Scott, hid from his pursuers, as Robin Hood is said to have concealed himself in Sherwood Forest.

Breadalbane, at the northern end of the national park, is the point where you enter the Highlands, and where you may see the Falls of Dochart as they cascade over rocks and around the island of Inchbuie, traditional burial place of the McNab clan. Argyll Forest, lying to the west, contains ancient trees, silent lochs and the 884 metre Ben Arthur, better known as The Cobbler. Its rocky summit sixty castles, twenty-five inhabited islands and, for connoisseurs of a dram, fourteen whisky distilleries.

The Isle of Islay alone has eight of those distilleries, and they produce world-famous, peat-flavoured malts such as Lagavulin, Ardbeg, Bruichladdich, Laphroaig and Caol Ila. The isle was formerly the home of the Lords of the Isles, once among the most powerful landowners in the British Isles. Nowadays the only possession of the descendants of the once mighty Clan Donald is the tiny isle of Cara, off the peninsula of Kintyre.

Other islands of the Inner Hebrides include the wild and mountainous Jura, Iona, Mull, Bute, Colonsay, Coll, Tiree, Easdale, Gigha (pronounced Geeya), Lismore, Luing and Seil. Each has its own distinctive character and some are more remote than others, but each can be reached with ease. The Isle of Mull, for example, is a short ferry ride from the mainland town of Oban. It's the third largest of Scotland's islands and is famous for the multicoloured frontages of the houses of its main town, Tobermory (the setting for the children's TV show *Balamory*), its bays and beaches and its spectacular wildlife including sea eagles.

Jura is a wild and mountainous island

Above: *Colonsay – island in the Inner Hebrides, ancestral home of the Clan MacNeill*

to the north of Islay and the home of a wonderfully rich whisky and herds of deer that vastly outnumber human residents. The isle, which is dominated by twin peaks known as the Paps of Jura, played host to the writer George Orwell as he struggled to finish his masterpiece *Nineteen Eighty-Four*. The Isle of Iona is a small crofting (farming) island with a notable past: it was here that Saint Columba arrived from Ireland to spread the gospel.

On the mainland of Argyll, there is much to explore. You could visit one of Scotland's finest stately homes, Inveraray Castle on the shores of Loch Fyne, or a

landmark built as a means of providing work for local stonemasons – McCaig's Tower overlooking Oban. And a visit to the region would not be complete without sampling some of its delicacies, including oysters and herring from the aforementioned Loch Fyne.

Enchanting glens and – perhaps – enchanted forests; golden beaches and tumbling rivers; lofty peaks and historic towns and villages – such is the region of Dundee and Angus, set on the east side of Scotland and greeting hordes of visitors each year.

The region's coastal towns have much to offer the curious tourist. At Dundee, Scotland's fourth largest city, there's the *RRS Discovery*, the ship in which Captain Robert Falcon Scott sailed to the Antarctic in 1901, and the Mills Observatory, the only full-time facility of its kind in the UK. The city's reputation for science is enhanced by Sensation, its science centre, which features interactive exhibitions, live shows and more.

You can learn about the lives of the Picts throughout the region, but one particular attraction – Pictavia in Brechin – is dedicated to bringing their era to life. Here one can discover the meanings of the Picts' carvings on stone, learn how and why they decorated their bodies and hear about their wars with Romans and Vikings. While in Brechin, you might want to wind down with a trip on the four-mile Caledonian Railway, preserved from Victorian times.

Set in the beautiful Strathmore Valley, Glamis Castle entices visitors to explore its splendour and its history. This fabulous building was the scene of Duncan's murder in *Macbeth*, and is said to contain a room where a nobleman played cards with the Devil. In Arbroath you'll find the ruins of Arbroath Abbey, known as the place from where the Declaration of Arbroath, a proclamation of Scottish independence, was sent in 1320.

If it's glorious landscapes you're after, make your way to the Angus Glens, not far from Dundee and the town of Angus. The five glens all run in the same direction, giving the impression of the fingers of a hand reaching up through the countryside to finish at the edge of the Cairngorms National Park. The scenery in Glenisla, Glen Prosen, Glen Clova, Glen Lethnot and Glen Esk encompasses heather-covered mountains and deep forests with rushing and tinkling streams.

While in the area, follow the Cateran Trail, which takes its name from the cattle thieves who once raided the rich lands of Strathardle, Glenshee and Glen Isla. Or perhaps you'd prefer to explore Glen Lethnot, where illicit whisky

distillers practised their craft, and follow the Whisky Road as it passes Clachan of Finnoch, a former Highland village that now lies in ruins.

And here we are at last in the Highlands region, a land of ancient beauty and gripping history; of dramatic vistas, lovely islands and beguiling culture. It's the part of Scotland that is most often pictured and written about in guide and travel books, and many visitors are persuaded to think that this region, of all regions, may be the 'real Scotland' – if that fascinating land can be said to exist.

The Highlands can be restful and exhausting, ravishing yet mysterious. There is a world to discover in this land, and you have an almost limitless choice when it comes to your method of discovery. If you're the 'active' type, water and winter sports abound, as do walking, cycling, climbing, golf and huntin', shootin' and fishin' opportunities. If you prefer the quieter life, a more leisurely exploration of the Highlands' wonders would be in order.

You could perhaps start in the gloomily beautiful, wild Glencoe, scene of the notorious massacre of the MacDonalds in 1692. Their sad story is told at the

Above: *The Highlands – mountain ranges dominate the region and include Britain's highest peak, Ben Nevis*

Glencoe Visitor Centre and Glencoe Folk Museum. Or you could walk the equally tragic turf of Culloden, where the last battle on British soil was fought in 1746 as the Jacobites fell to government troops.

In another infamous episode in the region's history, the Highlands Clearances of the eighteenth and nineteenth centuries, lowly inhabitants were driven from their homes by ruthless landowners. You can learn about this shameful slice of history at the Strathnaver Museum to the west of Thurso – almost as far north as you can go on the British mainland.

The country's largest national park,

that of the Cairngorms, offers miles of unspoiled mountain scenery, gorgeous lochs and purple heather-adorned glens of striking beauty – and many a physical activity to complement them. Of the multitude of isles lying off the Highlands' coast, the world-famous Skye has the awesome loveliness of the Cuillin hills and the Trotternish Ridge, over thirty kilometres of weird rock formations.

Perhaps we should leave the last word on the Highlands to the one place that will always be evoked when discussion turns to this region: Loch Ness. This thirty-kilometre long loch is much more than the reputed home of a celebrated water beast. It's also the largest lake by volume in Scotland, measuring 210 metres at its deepest. It's also a place brimming with historical associations, mysteries, natural wonders and – not surprisingly given its reputation – a plethora of welcoming places to stay and sup.

In some respects similar to the Highlands but in other ways startlingly different, the region known to the tourism professionals as Aberdeen City and Shire offers grand landscapes and majestic seascapes, awe-inspiring architecture and a long-standing maritime tradition.

There are royal connections too: Queen Victoria's love for Scotland inspired her husband, Prince Albert, to build Balmoral Castle as a holiday retreat in 'Royal' Deeside. It's still used by the royal family but you can visit when they're not there. The Victorian Heritage Trail takes you on a journey to some of the historic places associated with the monarchy. If you're still in a castle-visiting frame of mind, there are three hundred to choose from in this region, from cliff-top ruins to imposing countryside fortresses. And if you need some guidance, following the Castle Trail – the only one of its kind – will

lead you to seventeen of Aberdeenshire's most notable buildings.

Nature reserves abound, too. They range from Spey Bay near Elgin, the largest shingle beach in Scotland and home to a wide range of flora and fauna, to Muir of Dinnet near Ballater, an extensive area of birch wood, wetlands and heather moorland. There's also Glen Tanar, where visitors can explore a classic Caledonian pine forest and perhaps spot some of its wildlife.

The region supports a wide choice of golf and fishing locations, and for a taste of Highlands culture and history you could

Above:
Braemar Castle, Aberdeenshire – built in 1628, owned by the chief of Clan Farquharson

visit the Braemar Highland Heritage Centre or the Fraserburgh Heritage Centre, where four centuries of local history are on show in what was once a barrel store.

Aberdeen is Scotland's third largest urban centre, a busy city built of stone between the rivers Don and Dee. It boasts no fewer than three nicknames: the Granite City, the Grey City and the Silver City with the Golden Sands. Aberdeen is the centre of a strong industrial heritage, a thriving arts scene and a maritime tradition that dates back centuries. Fishing and shipbuilding have now been overtaken by the oil industry and a seaport as the main businesses of this vibrant city.

In Aberdeen there are plenty of art galleries and museums, including a Maritime Museum that tells the story of the city's long relationship with the sea. Follow the coast road north to Peterhead – the easternmost point of mainland Scotland – to find the Arbuthnot Museum and its displays of the town's fishing, shipping and whaling past.

Sitting on the very edge of Europe, fifty kilometres off the west coast, the Outer Hebrides is a chain of more than sixty alluring islands, fifteen of them inhabited.

The waters of the Minch, the Little Minch and the Sea of the Hebrides isolate the islands from the Scottish mainland and help them to retain their special ambience and culture. Fewer than thirty thousand people live on these enchanting rocks, where Gaelic predominates as the spoken language and where much employment centres on crofting, fishing, weaving and – happily for you, dear reader – tourism.

These islands offer the visitor a mild climate, white beaches pounded by mighty Atlantic waves, dark moorlands and towering peaks. There's wildlife aplenty and ancient cultural marvels have been preserved right into the twenty-first century.

Right at the top of the chain lies Lewis, the largest of the Western Isles. Life revolves around the town of Stornoway, the largest settlement in the islands, but splendid isolation can also be found here in the desolate peat bogs and on the beaches. Among the top attractions are the fifty standing stones of Callanais, which date from around 3000BC.

Some of Scotland's best beaches can be found on Harris, which is joined to Lewis and is itself divided into two by a narrow isthmus. South Uist is an isle of contrasts, its eastern side being mountainous while on the west sandy beaches are backed by dunes and grassy plains. Visitors to North Uist arriving by ferry at the former fishing port of Lochmaddy often set off in search of the huge chambered burial cairn of Barpa Langais.

The small island of Benbecula, flat, low-lying and sprinkled with tiny lochs, lies between North and South Uist. Visitors to Barra, the most southerly of the inhabited islands and noted for its beauty, will find their plane landing on one of the world's most unusual airstrips, on the beach at Cockle Strand. The pilot will first ensure the tide is out.

The archipelago of Orkney is to be found off the north-east coast of Scotland, with the nearest solid ground being sixteen kilometres from the town of Caithness. This chain consists of around seventy islands, twenty of which are inhabited; the earliest inhabitants moved in approximately 8,500 years ago. The main island – known simply as Mainland – is Scotland's sixth largest.

Orkney, settled by Norse peoples in the ninth century, annexed to the Scottish Crown in 1472 and now with a population of less than twenty thousand, has some of the oldest and best-preserved

Above: *Italian Chapel on Lamb Holm, Orkney – built by Italian prisoners of war during World War II*

Neolithic sites in Europe. This truly is a magical region in which pristine beaches combine with fascinating culture, heritage and wildlife to offer the visitor an unforgettable experience.

The Orkney Mainland is divided into two parts, East and West, and has Kirkwall as its administrative centre. The town is home to the famous Highland Park whisky distillery, founded in 1798 by the infamous smuggler Magnus Eunson, as well as the St Magnus (no relation) Cathedral, known as the Light in the North and established by the Viking Earl Rognvald in 1137.

The tranquil East Mainland is low-

Right: *St Ninian's Isle, Shetland – connected to Mainland by a five hundred metre tombolo, or sand spit*

lying and offers attractive sandy beaches as well as the vertiginous cliffs of the Mull Head RSPB Reserve. The smaller islands of Copinsay (owned, together with Corn Holm, Black Holm and Ward Holm, by the RSPB), Burray and South Ronaldsay can be easily reached from East Mainland, the latter two via causeways called Churchill Barriers built during World War II.

West Mainland is easily its neighbour's equal, featuring as it does luscious scenery and fabulous wildlife. A prime attraction is its UNESCO World Heritage Site, the Heart of Neolithic Orkney. This stunning site consists of Maeshowe, a large chambered tomb; two ceremonial stone circles, the Stones of Stenness and the Ring of Brodgar; and the famed Stone Age settlement of Skara Brae, along with a number of unexplored burial, ceremonial and settlement areas. Stromness, West Mainland's largest town, is notable for its museum, its arts centre and its narrow winding streets and alleys.

Orkney's Outer Islands are in the main low-lying, with gently rolling landscapes, heather moorlands and lochs to explore. The main inhabited islands are North Ronaldsay, Papa Westray, Westray, Shapinsay, Gairsay, Stronsay, Wyre, Egilsay, Eday and Sanday.

Our tour of Scotland and its isles must end at its most far-flung outposts, the islands of Shetland. Lying eighty kilometres to the north-east of Orkney and populated by twenty-two thousand souls, Shetland is an archipelago of one large island (again, simply called Mainland) and a further fifteen inhabited isles and around a hundred uninhabited ones with rugged coastlines, geological complexities to delight the expert and landscapes typified by low, rolling hills.

This is a captivating group of islands. Shetland, for many centuries a Norse possession, did not become part of Scotland until the fifteenth century, and it retains a unique blend of Norse and Scottish culture. The Shetlandic dialect, based on Insular Scots but containing distinct traces of Scandinavian languages, is still spoken here, and the mixed heritage is reflected in events like the annual Up Helly Aa fire festival.

Shetland's largest town, Lerwick, is to be found on the east side of Mainland. Here you can discover Fort Charlotte, a pentagonal artillery fort and garrison that was built to defend the Sound of Bressay during the Anglo-Dutch wars of the seventeenth and eighteenth centuries. The secrets of Up Helly Aa are revealed in a Lerwick exhibition, and the town is also home to the Shetland Museum and Archives, set within a restored nineteenth century dock.

Unst is Britain's most northerly inhabited island and, like many others in the region, a major breeding ground for seabirds including gannets, guillemots and kittiwakes. Fair Isle, famous for its woollen jumpers, lies midway between Shetland and Orkney and is thus Britain's most remote inhabited island.

Papa Stour is a small island to the west of Mainland and is home to a community of about thirty people. Popular with walkers, it can be reached via plane or a forty-five minute ferry journey. Half an hour on a ferry from Mainland will take you to Whalsay, an island whose history is rooted in fishing, nowadays a multi-million pound industry. Shetland's most easterly outposts are the Out Skerries, three minuscule islands to the east of Whalsay. The Scandinavian connection is as strong here as anywhere in Shetland, for the islets' Bund Skerry lighthouse is a mere three hundred kilometres from the coast of Norway.

For this brief survey of Scotland it's been necessary to omit countless places and experiences that would, if visited, prove truly memorable. It's only to be hoped that these few words will inspire you to seek out the best the country has to offer – and return again and again to search for new wonders.

Culture an' a' That

As we've already seen, Scotland is a unique country in many respects – historically, geographically and architecturally, to name but three. We'll go on to see how this small nation has managed to produce many more men and women of genius than anyone could expect of it, and explore some more of its natural singularities, but in this chapter we focus on another distinct aspect of Scotland: its culture.

In terms of many facets of its life, Scotland stands apart from other nations. Peculiarities of its food and drink cannot be found anywhere else in the world. Its languages, its customs and its traditional dress stand alone. Its arts – music, poetry and other forms of literature – have long been acclaimed for their extraordinariness and splendour. Its canon of myth and legend, and its sporting life, have a flavour all of their own.

These unique facets of Scotland have been born of a number of nurturing factors: the nature of its peoples, geographical peculiarities of the place, historical, political and religious influences, the climate, natural resources and many more intangible effects. How, exactly? We are about to see how a country of only five million people can produce so much that is so special.

Any discussion of Scotland and its place in the world will eventually turn to its cuisine and especially its contribution

to the world's drinks culture, so it seems natural to start this chapter with an examination of the country's food and drink. And haggis is the traditional starting point for discussions of this nature.

The great chieftain o' the pudding race, as Robert Burns memorably put it, is in fact a small, elusive beast with two legs shorter than the others, making them ideal for when the haggis is running round mountains, which is what it mostly does. At least that's what you'll be told at some point. In fact the haggis – prepare yourself for the unadorned truth – consists of the minced liver, heart and lungs of whichever unlucky animal's turn it was (could be sheep, cow, pig or sometimes even deer), mixed with oatmeal, suet, onions and spices and boiled in the stomach of the animal in question. The contents are released from their fleshy prison to be eaten, traditionally accompanied by tatties and neeps (potatoes and turnips).

If it sounds revolting, well, you're not

Centre: *Highland cattle – hardy breed that yields leaner meat than many other beef cattle*

the first to think that. The truth is haggis tastes a lot better, an awful lot better, than it sounds. It is truly one of the world's great national dishes. So highly did the great poet Burns regard the haggis that he chose to address one thus:

> *Fair fa' your honest sonsie face,*
> *Great chieftain o' the pudding race!*
> *Aboon them a' yet tak your place,*
> *Painch, tripe, or thairm:*
> *Weel are ye wordy o' a grace*
> *As lang's my arm.*

If you're struggling with the language, just take it from me that Burns was a haggis fan, and he unwittingly launched a tradition according to which his *Address to a Haggis* is recited with great ceremony at each Burns supper celebrating his memory.

Haggis grabs the headlines, but there's much more to the nation's food than this delicious dish. Cereals like barley and oats, for example, play a central role in traditional Scottish cuisine, with the latter particularly prominent. Where would a gift shop in Scotland be without its display of oatcakes? In former times baked in triangular form on a girdle – an iron plate placed on the fire – oatcakes are now mass-produced and will often be offered to visitors to be eaten at the end of a meal with cheese.

Porridge is another oat product – a healthy product, too – that visitors to Scotland may come across for the first time. It was traditionally made by soaking the oats overnight and boiling them for breakfast, with the necessary stirring to remove the lumps carried out with a spirtle (wooden stick). Salt was added if it was wanted, but nowadays you'll find

around the world. This buttery biscuit is said to have originated with Mary, Queen of Scots, an avid muncher of a delicacy of her times called Petticoat Tails.

Every corner of Scotland is the proud producer of cheeses, and some of the most ancient that can still be found include Crowdie (soft, rolled in oatmeal, first produced by the Vikings), Caboc (made in the western Highlands, also rolled in oatmeal), Lanark Blue (made with sheep's milk) and Bishop Kennedy (soft, unpasteurised, washed in malt whisky).

Scottish farmers really come into their own when it comes to meat. Some of the world's best beef, lamb and pork come from animals raised on the country's lush pastures, with beef in pride of place. Native cattle breeds such as the Aberdeen Angus and the Highland are justly known the world over, and they're complemented by meat from breeds such as the Belted Galloway and Beef Shorthorn.

You shouldn't leave Scotland with tasting black pudding. An ingredient of many a breakfast, this is another way, like haggis, of ensuring that not much of an animal goes to waste. It's a mixture of pigs' blood, fat, oats, barley and spices, stuffed into a length of intestine and sliced when ready to cook.

milk, sugar or syrup being added with barely a guilty look from the perpetrator.

Two further choice dishes made from oats are cranachan (oats mixed with raspberries, whipped cream and perhaps a tot of whisky, eaten as a dessert) and skirlie (oats and onion cooked together and served as an addition to minced meat and tatties).

The gift shops mentioned earlier will, it's certain, also stock some shortbread, a Scottish delicacy that has made its way

Above: A wee dram – First Minister Alex Salmond visits the Glenglassaugh distillery, which restarted production in 2008 after a gap of twenty-two years

When it comes to game, in which Scotland specialises, you'll find yourself paying a handsome price for grouse, but other game birds such as pheasant can be highly rewarding. Venison, too, should be sampled when found, and so much the better if the meat on your plate came from a deer that once roamed free, although farm-raised varieties are not to be sniffed at.

Where better to end this short round-up of Scottish delicacies than in the nation's seas and rivers, source of so much that is good about the country? Foodies have been known to travel vast distances to savour Scotland's fish and seafood, the envy of producers the world over.

You may be lucky enough to try your luck at catching a salmon or trout for your dinner. If not, you're still in for a treat if you have these delicacies set before you. Salmon farms are fairly widespread nowadays, but the wild fish can be caught in famed rivers like the Spey, the Tweed, the Dee and the Tay, and many another like them.

The freshwater salmon is the king of fish, rightly prized for the robustness of its meat and the delicacy of its flavour. The trout is a relation, but not a poor one. Brown trout caught in a river can be fabulous, while the sea trout is a treat. Rainbow trout are also often farmed.

Scotland is famous for herring and its haddock, often to be found in chip shops, is a delight. But perhaps Scotland's culinary crowning glory is its seafood.

Crab, lobster, langoustine from the lochs of the west coast, farmed scallops and oysters swallowed with a little lemon juice are all especially toothsome. And you will have to go a very long way indeed to beat a succulent mussel cultivated on the west coast. Scotland says: don't leave our shores until you've tried them.

In matters of a more liquid kind, Scotland once again leads the way. It's well nigh impossible to think of a country anywhere in the world to which the fame

of its whisky – derived from uisge beatha, Gaelic for water of life – has not spread. And the beauty of whisky is that it's not just one national drink but hundreds.

Scotch whisky is produced in distilleries all over the country and each has its peculiarities, which result in a drink that can be different in character to that of a producer a few miles down the road and a world away from the whiskies of another region. The difference might be the result of the shape of the still in which a whisky is distilled, the cask in which it's aged, the nature of the water used or even the local countryside.

It might have been influenced by the fuel used to dry the germinating barley, the location of the distillery – inland, on a seashore or elsewhere – or any of a number of other external influences. It might be that the Scotch in your glass is a blend of single malt whiskies (each from one distillery) with grain whiskies, and it may be none the worse for that. The world's best-selling Scotch whiskies are blends.

To appreciate the complexities of Scotch, you need to know how it's produced. In the production of a malt whisky, three natural ingredients are used: water, malted barley and yeast. The

first process is the malting of the barley, in which it's steeped in water and then spread out on a malting floor, where it germinates. This produces starch that can be converted into soluble sugars, which are then turned into alcohol. When the barley starts to sprout, the germination is stopped by drying the barley in a kiln. Here the character of a whisky can be influenced by the burning of peat to produce the heat.

When it's dry, the malt is ground (becoming 'grist') and mixed with hot water in a mash tun. Sugars from the malt dissolve and produce the liquid ('wort')

that is used in the fermentation. The wort is fermented through the addition of yeast in big vessels ('washbacks'). The yeast turns the sugar in the wort to alcohol and the distiller is left with a liquid (the 'wash') that contains about eight per cent alcohol by volume.

Now comes the distillation, which is carried out in copper stills: a wash still and a spirit still. The wash is heated first, resulting in alcohol vapours rising and passing through condensers, in which they return to liquid form. The spirit that results ('low wines') is then distilled again in the spirit still, and what comes out is collected.

Our whisky is far from finished at this stage. It must be placed in oak casks and matured for at least three years before it has the right to call itself Scotch whisky. As it matures it will gain colouring and absorb influences from outside, adding further characteristics.

So there, after at least three years but often after a much longer period than that, we have a single malt whisky. To show how enormously Scotch whisky can vary in taste, aroma and colour, let's examine whiskies from each of the five producing regions: Lowland, Campbeltown, Islay, Highland and Speyside.

Glenkinchie is a Lowland whisky produced near Edinburgh. The twelve-year-old is a typical Lowland malt, fresh and light in character with a sweet aroma and a hint of peat. You may detect notes of lemon and grass. Glenkinchie's fourteen-year-old is double-matured in sherry casks, giving it a slightly deeper flavour.

There are now just three distilleries producing Campbeltown single malts on the Kintyre peninsula. At Springbank, Hazelburn twelve-year-old gets its delicate character through being distilled three times. No peat is used, which means the whisky is light, flowery and fruity,

even slightly nutty.

Eight distilleries can be found on the Isle of Islay. Lagavulin is one, and its standard sixteen-year-old is distinguished by its strong peaty flavour and overtones of iodine – the result of the distillery's proximity to the seashore with its deposits of seaweed. This is a dark, intense, love-it-or-hate-it whisky, and perhaps not one for the beginner.

Highland malts come from distilleries spread out over an enormous area of the Highlands and islands. One of the most famous is from Glenmorangie, where hard water filtered down the ages through limestone is used in the fermentation. The ten-year-old whisky, light in colour, is creamy and fruity, and your nose might detect hints of apple, lemon and nectarine.

The final region, Speyside, is home to over half of Scotland's distilleries. Macallan, another world-famous producer, has a superb ten-year-old in its range. Matured in sherry casks, it's a light malt with clean but sweet flavours – some tasters insist they can detect the taste of vanilla fudge.

You're now almost fully equipped to start an exploration of Scotch whisky that will doubtless be a lifelong delight. One question remains: how should you drink whisky? There's no definitive answer apart from 'the way you enjoy it', but you could maybe take a tip from the Scottish connoisseurs who add nothing to their whisky but a drop of water.

Scotland offers the thirsty much more than just whisky, of course. One carbonated soft drink beloved of the Scots, Irn-Bru, sometimes has the impertinence to challenge whisky for the title of national drink, while the country can boast some excellence mineral waters – one is even said by researchers to give its drinkers a younger appearance. But any survey of Scottish food and drink would be incomplete without a look at the nation's beer.

They've been brewing beer in Scotland for about five thousand years, and Scots remain devoted to this natural restorative. Many a native drinker will swear by his pint of lager, but brewers also produce a number of varieties of ale. These are often labelled using the traditional 'shilling' system, which roughly means that a beer called light (60/- or sixty shilling) would contain under 3.5 per cent alcohol by volume; heavy (70/-) would have between 3.5 and four per cent; export (80/-) would contain between four and 5.5 per cent; and wee heavy (90/-) would be over six per cent. Scottish ales tend to be darker, sweeter and less hop-flavoured than those in England and Wales. Here are just a few you might be lucky enough to find.

Deuchars IPA (3.8 per cent alcohol by volume) is a gold-coloured beer with a crisp bitterness, while Caledonian 80/- (4.1 per cent abv) is brown, smooth and creamy. Orkney Best (3.6 per cent abv) is pale, refreshing and easy-drinking. Pentland IPA from Stewart Brewing (3.9 per cent abv) is a moderately bitter, dry ale, while bottled Belhaven Scottish Ale

Above: *Scottish salmon – the king of fish, prized for the delicacy of its flavour*

(available in 3.9 and 5.2 per cent styles) has a distinctive malty and nutty flavour.

Cheers, or as your drinking companions might say, slàinte mhath.

Which leads us on nicely to the subject of the languages spoken in Scotland. 'Slàinte mhath' ('good health'– a rough pronunciation guide would be slanzh'va) is a nice example of Scottish Gaelic, one of the tongues encountered in Scotland and its islands. The other two main languages are English and Scots.

Be assured, wary traveller: English – or at least one of its Scottish English dialects – can be heard anywhere in the country, but for a proper immersion in Scotland it's good to know that other tongues are spoken.

Scottish Gaelic, which like modern Irish and Manx developed out of Old Irish, is almost entirely exclusive to the western Highlands and the Hebrides. Scots is a different matter. Otherwise known as Doric or Lallans, it's the national name for the Scottish dialects that are spoken throughout the Lowlands and Northern Isles. It has many local varieties, each of which has its own distinctive characteristics, and can be heard in the Borders, Dumfries and Galloway, Glasgow, Edinburgh and the Lothians, Fife, Dundee, Tayside, Caithness, Aberdeen, the North-East, Orkney and Shetland.

Scots was the language used by Robert Burns in his celebrated poetry. It's the language of the people, spoken in homes and pubs, in the street and in shops. It's the everyday tongue of Scotland.

Just as a first-time visitor to the country may sometimes be hard-pressed to discern what a Scot is saying in English due to the wide variety of regional and local accents, so it may sometimes be difficult to understand when someone is using Scots. The following glossary, which picks out a few common Scots words, some Gaelic, some dialect words and some others used in this book, may help a little.

Scots and Scottish Gaelic glossary

Scots	English
Aback	Behind
Auld	Old
Bairn	Child
Bannock	Oatmeal biscuit
Bawbees	Money
Ben	Mountain
Brae	Slope of a hill, river bank
Burn	Stream
Canny	Careful
Close	Common stairwell in tenement building
Crannog	Ancient loch dwelling
Croft	Small farm
Dram	Glass of whisky
Dreich	Dull, miserable (of weather)
Gae, gang	Go
Glen	Valley
Gloaming	Dusk
Greet	Weep, sob
Haar	Sea fog
Heid	Head
Inver	River mouth
Keek	Glance, peep
Ken	Know
Kirk	Church
Loch	Lake
Lochan	Small lake
Lum	Chimney
Machair	Low-lying, grassy coastal plain
Messages	Shopping
Mind	Remember
Neep	Turnip
Oxter	Armpit
Peely-wally	Pale, sickly
Reiver	Robber, cattle raider
Sgian dubh	Knife worn with Highland dress
Skelp	Strike, slap
Skerry	Small rocky island
Stramash	Commotion, brawl
Pend	Passageway through building
Tattie	Potato
Wain/wean	Child, infant
Wee	Little
Wynd	Lane between houses
Wheesht	Hush, quiet!

This is just a tiny selection, but arm yourself with a bit of Scottish vocabulary and you'll be halfway to understanding the country.

The sgian dubh mentioned above – translated from the Gaelic it can mean black or hidden knife – is traditionally tucked into the stocking of a man in Highland dress. And that, of course, means the kilt, and it means tartan. It means Scotland's most recognisable style of dress.

Tartan was being worn in central Europe many centuries ago, but as far as Scotland is concerned it originated in the Highlands, where plants, mosses and berries would be used to dye wool before it was spun and woven into the sort of patterns we're familiar with. It's not known how long tartan has been worn in Scotland, but it was certainly mentioned in 1538.

Clanspeople at that time tended to wear different patterns and weaves according to the custom of their area, but in the eighteenth century the Highland regiments of the army started to standardise their tartans. The idea that different tartans might represent different clans and families took hold in the Victorian era, and from that beginning sprang a mighty industry.

If you want to wear a tartan it's really up to you which one you choose, although if you're keen to follow the standardisation initiated by those Victorians, a little research will be needed to find to which clan you or your forebears belong.

Like tartan, the kilt was not a Scottish invention, but it first appeared in the Highlands as the féileadh mór ('big kilt') or plaid. This was a full-length garment around five metres in length, of which the upper half could be worn as a cloak draped over the shoulder or head, depending on the weather. It was belted at the waist and the lower half looked more or less like the modern kilt. At night the whole garment could be wrapped round the body to provide warm sleeping attire – the word plaid meant blanket.

It was in the eighteenth century that the kilt became more like the pleated garment resembling a skirt that we know today. Once again, it was our friends in the Highland regiments who provided the impetus for this innovation. The kilt is today worn as everyday wear or as part of formal attire for special occasions.

It's impossible to talk about the kilt without mentioning the sporran. These handy pouches, suspended on chains or leather at the front of the kilt, serve as wallets and receptacles for any items needed as the wearer goes about his business. They're normally made of

leather or fur and their ornamentation varies widely – it can depend on the formality of the occasion.

And to the perennial tiresome question to kilt wearers of whether they wear anything under the kilt, there's only one possible response: guess.

The choice of what to wear, as we've seen, depends on the type of occasion, and the type of occasion often depends on the date. There are two very notable dates in the Scottish calendar that are especially worthy of mention: December 31 and January 25.

Many countries celebrate the New Year, but none celebrate it in quite the same way as the Scots. Their Hogmanay celebrations take festivities to a level all of their own, and there are also peculiarly

Centre: *Shinty – now played mainly in the Highlands*

Scottish customs associated with the event that are found in few other places.

One notable custom practised widely is that of first-footing. This involves being the first person to set foot in a household after midnight – in other words the first visitor of the new year – and offering gifts to the householders. The presents may consist of coal, shortbread, whisky or black bun, a kind of fruit cake. This all brings good luck to the household. In turn, the hosts offer their visitors food and drink, and so the Hogmanay festivities continue. Traditionally, it's a good omen if a tall, dark man is the first-footer, while redheads and blonds can mean the reverse.

Hogmanay in Scotland is a serious business. Cities like Edinburgh hold massive street parties on New Year's Eve and alcohol flows in great volumes before the chimes of midnight, when arms will be linked and *Auld Lang Syne* will be sung. Nothing much gets done on the first day of the new year, and it's worth noting that January 2 is also a public holiday in Scotland.

Burns Night, celebrating the birthday of the national poet Robert Burns on January 25, is another occasion for letting the hair down. Burns Suppers are held throughout the land as a way of venerating

the most Scottish of literary giants.

We've already seen how the haggis traditionally served at these events is addressed with great reverence in the words of Burns, after it's been accompanied to the table by a bagpiper. A Burns Supper, which usually follows a strict programme, is also the occasion of speeches, toasts, recitations, more toasts, songs and sometimes a further toast for good luck. It's what the great man would have wanted, say the Scots.

Another Scottish special occasion at which kilts are worn strays into the area of sports. The gatherings known as Highland games, which take place during the summer months, celebrate the country's culture and heritage and are often witnessed by huge crowds. These events are a mixture of heavyweight sports, dance competitions, foot races and massed bagpipe bands as well as piping and drumming contests.

Highland dance, whose current form evolved during the nineteenth and twentieth centuries, shows off the complex footwork and the dedication of its practitioners, who practise over many years to attain high levels of competence. Competitive in the extreme – it's recognised as a sport by Sportscotland –

it requires stamina and strength as well as technical excellence, for performers dance on the balls of their feet. At the Cowal Gathering in Dunoon, the world's largest Highland games, 650 dancers compete in the World Highland Dance Championships.

The 'heavy' events in Highland games are a test of strength and character of which the best-known example is the caber toss. Competitors hoist aloft a long pine pole and try to toss it so that it turns end over end – it sounds a lot easier than it is. The stone put event is similar to the shot put seen in athletics meets, except that a large stone is used. The weight throw involves projecting a metal ball as far as possible, while in the 'weight for height' contest competitors attempt to heave a fifty-six pound weight over a horizontal bar.

All of these competitions lead us to consider the matter of Scotland's voracious appetite for sports. Scotland plays an important role in most of the big international sports, and has been the major force in bringing many other events to world prominence.

The country is known as the place where golf developed into its modern form, and St Andrews, as we have seen, is still regarded as the home of the game. The Scots' passion for golf can be gauged from the sheer number of courses that dot the countryside, both inland and on the coasts. The country has produced many top international players and the world's biggest competition is still the Open Championship, which started at Prestwick in Scotland in 1860 and continues to visit the nation's challenging links courses.

Football, or soccer to our North American cousins, is another huge passion. Scotland boasts the world's second oldest football association and thriving professional and semi-professional leagues. Its national team and top clubs have proved themselves on international stages, and to get a flavour of how brightly the football flame burns in Scots' hearts, a visit to a major domestic fixture is essential. Old Firm matches between Glasgow's top two clubs, Rangers and Celtic, are among the most fiercely contested events in any sport, and the rivalry is mirrored in Edinburgh, where Hibernian (or Hibs) and Heart of Midlothian (Hearts) vie for supremacy.

In Edinburgh you will also find Murrayfield, home of the Scottish rugby union team. International rugby made its debut in Edinburgh in 1871, when Scotland beat England in front of four thousand people, and the game's first league structure also sprang up in the country. Rugby is most popular in the Borders region, from where crowds flock to Murrayfield to watch Scotland take on its international rivals in the Six Nations tournament.

Other sports, less well known internationally, owe their existence to Scotland and are practised with enthusiasm within the country. One of these is curling, which is thought to have been invented in medieval times.

This is the sport you've seen on TV during Winter Olympic Games. Two teams of four players take turns to slide heavy, polished granite stones across a sheet of ice towards the 'house', a circular target marked on the ice. Points are scored for the stones that come to rest closest to the house. The curler can make the stone moved in a curved path by making it turn, and as it glides towards its target, sweepers use brooms to slow down or accelerate its movement. Scotland has produced many top international curlers over the years.

Another popular ball game in Scotland is shinty, or camanachd, to give it its Gaelic name. This is a truly ancient sport

thought to predate Christianity, and has a lot in common with the Irish pastime of hurling.

Shinty has certain features in common with hockey and ice hockey, but there are big differences. A shinty player is allowed to play the ball in the air and with both sides of his stick, or caman, which is made of wood and slanted on both sides. The caman can be used to block and tackle, and players can also tackle using shoulder-to-shoulder contact. Shinty is now played mainly in the Highlands, and is reported widely in the region's press.

Above: *Wembley Wizards – the Scottish football team who beat world champions England 3-2 at Wembley in 1967, a victory that has lived long in the nation's memory*

When most people contemplating paying a visit to Scotland think of its music, one instrument will inevitably spring to mind: the bagpipes. It's true the pipes are the country's national

Above: *Curling – Scotland has produced many top international players over the years*

instrument, but there's much more to music in Scotland than the haunting skirl of a lone piper or the stirring strains of a marching pipe band.

Different types of bagpipes are known throughout the world as well as in Scotland. The Lowland pipes are popular but the Highland bagpipe is probably the best known. Its music, which has deep roots in Scotland's Gaelic cultural history,

has two main styles: ceòl mór (big music) and ceòl beag (little music). In ceòl mór or pibroch – the classical music of the bagpipes, if you like – the pipes are played by a single piper. The music tends to be slow, stately and complex, lasting several minutes, and pibrochs are often written for solemn events or occasions like salutes, gatherings and laments. Ceòl beag refers to dance music such as jigs, reels,

CULTURE AN' A' THAT

strathspeys and slow airs.

The pipes look complicated, and to an extent they are. The piper blows into a pipe to keep a bag full of a reservoir of air, which then escapes through four other pipes. Three of these pipes are drones, which play steady notes; the other is the chanter, which is fingered by the piper to produce a tune in the key of B flat.

The other national instruments of Scotland are the fiddle and clàrsach, or small harp. The former comes into its own when it's playing lively, uptempo dance tunes, while the harp was in the past sometimes used to lull people to sleep. Nevertheless, it plays an important part in traditional Scottish dance music.

You'll also often hear an accordion being played if you chance upon a ceilidh, a social gathering at which there'll be music, dancing, laughs and a marvellous community spirit. It's not a problem if you don't know the steps to any of the dances: someone will help you out, and there's sometimes a caller to guide you through the mysteries of jigs, reels, waltzes and strathspeys. A pub is often the place to go if you want to hear Scottish traditional music being played without having to learn a dance or two.

Another area in which Scotland has made a mark on the world is that of contemporary music. In the field of contemporary folk – a meld of rock and traditional music that combines the instruments and feel of the two genres – bands such as the Peatbog Faeries and Salsa Celtica stand out, and the annual Celtic Connections festival in Glasgow celebrates Celtic music and its connections as they're played across the globe. The Battlefield Band are another act worth catching, as are Ceilidh Minogue, even if it's only for the name.

Leading practitioners of contemporary popular music have been playing their way into the hearts of the world's music lovers for decades. They include such past and present bands and musicians as the Proclaimers, Big Country, Ian Anderson of Jethro Tull, Annie Lennox, the Average White Band, the Cocteau Twins, Del Amitri, Simple Minds, Aztec Camera, the Jesus and Mary Chain, Primal Scream and Emeli Sandé.

Robert Burns was a dab hand at composing songs, although he is of course best known as Scotland's greatest purveyor of the written word, a poet of immense fame who continues to influence Scottish literature to this day. Burns wrote

Far Right: *Sir Walter Scott – writer of many classics of English literature*

in both Scots and English, and he wrote verse in many styles: romantic, epic, philosophical and humorous to name just a few. We will explore the life of Burns in detail in the following chapter. Here it's more appropriate to quote some of this best-loved works that have become just as familiar as his *Auld Lang Syne*.

Tam O' Shanter is an epic poem that tells the tale of a man who tarries in a tavern and witnesses weird visions on his way home. He sees:

> *A winnock-bunker in the east,*
> *There sat auld Nick, in shape o' beast;*
> *A towzie tyke, black, grim, and large,*
> *To gie them music was his charge:*
> *He screw'd the pipes and gart them skirl,*
> *Till roof and rafters a' did dirl.*

Never mind, Tam. We've all been there. Burns speaks in a very different tone in *A Red, Red Rose*, written in 1795 and expressing egalitarian ideas of society. It's otherwise known as *Is There Honest Poverty*.

> *A prince can mak a belted knight,*
> *A marquis, duke, an' a' that;*
> *But an honest man's abon his might,*
> *Gude faith, he maunna fa' that!*

> *For a' that, an' a' that,*
> *Their dignities, an' a' that;*
> *The pith o' sense, an' pride o' worth,*
> *Are higher rank that a' that.*

If you want to dig deeper into the works of Burns, you'll be glad to hear you can download a smartphone app with a database of every one of his poems. If you don't have a smartphone, you can content yourself at the annual Burns an' a' That! Festival, held every year in his home county of Ayrshire, or visit one of the many attractions that celebrate the life of one of Scotland's great heroes.

Scotland has produced many other writers of great renown. The greatest of recent years is undoubtedly JK Rowling, author of the Harry Potter books that sell in their millions worldwide. Among other modern authors to have stirred the imaginations of readers beyond Scotland's borders are Ian Rankin, whose fictional detective Rebus haunts the wynds and pubs of Edinburgh, and Iain Banks, the author of acclaimed mainstream fiction under that name and science fiction under the name of Iain M Banks.

In 2004, Edinburgh became the first UNESCO City of Literature, and it's great fun to explore the city in search of its literary connections. Here you can find the birthplaces of Robert Louis Stevenson, the creator of *Treasure Island*, and Muriel Spark, whose *The Prime of Miss Jean Brodie* is considered an essential Edinburgh novel. You can also see the home of Sir Walter Scott, whose works like *The Lady of the Lake*, *Ivanhoe*, *Rob Roy* and *The Heart of Midlothian* are considered classics of English literature. The mighty Scott Monument in central Edinburgh commemorates his memory. There's also the annual Edinburgh International Book Festival to consider if you're a true book person.

Study of Scottish literature need not stop with the names already mentioned. Others like JM Barrie, John Buchan, Kenneth Grahame, Sir Arthur Conan Doyle, Carol Ann Duffy, RM Ballantyne, Irvine Welsh, James Kelman and thousands of others have perpetuated the country's proud tradition, and will continue to do so.

The fabulous folklore and legends of Scotland are another draw that continues to attract visitors. Where, for instance, would the country's tourism business be without the presence of a certain beast said to frequent the depths

Right: *Loch Ness – home of a fabled water beast, it contains more fresh water than all the lakes in England and Wales combined*

of Loch Ness?

Nessie, or the Loch Ness Monster to give the animal her full title, first appeared as long ago as the seventh century, when Adomnán described her in his *Life of Saint Columba*. The saint, he wrote, came across the burial of a man who had reportedly been attacked by a water beast while swimming in the River Ness. The saint promptly lured the beast out of her lair only to fill her with terror by making the sign of the cross and commanding her to retreat.

Interest in Nessie increased in the 1930s with the appearance of blurred photographs of what looked vaguely like a plesiosaur – a marine reptile of ancient times. Since then, expeditions have combed the loch for signs of the elusive animal, with far from conclusive results. Sightings have been judged a mixture of hoax and wishful thinking. But then Nessie, being a rather shy creature, would want us to believe that, wouldn't she?

Nessie is not the only 'monster' to abide in Scottish lochs. Mòrag is said to inhabit Loch Morar, also in the Highlands. The best-known sighting occurred in 1969, when two men in a boat disturbed the poor humped beast and, so they say, shot her with a rifle. So perhaps Mòrag is no longer with us, but what about Mucsheilche, the water beast of Loch Maree? A Mr Banks of Letterewe was so determined to catch her in the nineteenth century that he attempted to drain the loch and poison her with quicklime. What of Seileag, who is said to inhabit Loch Shiel?

The folklore of Scotland abounds in

mysterious creatures, spirits and beings. There's the kelpie, the water horse said to haunt lochs and rivers. There are the selkies, capable of transforming themselves from human to seal form and back again. There are the blue men of Minch, blue-skinned beings who searched the waters between Lewis and the mainland for sailors to drown. There is the Bean-Nighe or washerwoman, a fairy who sits by a river or pool washing the clothes of those about to die.

Real, or the product of the Scottish gift for invention and narrative? The decision is up to you, but it must not be taken lightly.

Great Scots

For a country with a small population, which was even smaller in days gone by, Scotland has an outstanding record of producing great thinkers, writers, artists, scientists, engineers, politicians, sports people, entertainers … the list goes on. Here are a few of them.

John Logie Baird
Engineer, inventor of the world's first practical, publicly demonstrated television

Born the son of a clergyman in Helensburgh in 1888, John Logie Baird showed early signs of his potential, rigging up a telephone exchange so he could communicate with friends across the street. He was studying at the Glasgow and West of Scotland Technical College when World War I broke out but ill health, which dogged him for most of his life, meant he was unfit for service. Working instead as superintendent engineer of the Clyde Valley Electrical Power Company, he set up in business after the war.

Moving to England's south coast, Baird pursued an aim previously followed by other scientists without great success: the creation of a television. By 1924 he had succeeded in transmitting an indistinct image a few feet, and two years later, in a London attic room, he gave the first demonstration of true television to fifty scientists.

Improvements followed swiftly. In 1927 Baird demonstrated television transmission between London and Glasgow and formed the Baird Television Development Company. And the following year saw the first transatlantic transmission between London and New York, the first to a ship in mid-Atlantic and the first showings of both colour and stereoscopic television.

In 1929, the German post office allowed him to develop an experimental TV service based on his mechanical system. Eventually, electronic systems, developed chiefly by Marconi, superseded Baird's system. He died in Bexhill-on-Sea in 1946.

Alexander Graham Bell

Scientist, engineer, inventor of the first practical telephone

Above: *Alexander Graham Bell – awarded the first US patent for a telephone in 1876*

Bell was born in 1847 in Edinburgh to a father who was an authority on elocution, and when he was sixteen he began to study the mechanics of speech. With his family, he emigrated to Canada

Centre: *Robert the Bruce – succeeded in regaining independence for Scotland*

in 1870 and the following year moved to the United States to teach.

He pioneered a system developed by his father and called visible speech, and in 1872 founded a school in Boston to train teachers of the deaf. Interested in the idea of transmitting speech, Bell developed a simple receiver that turned electricity into sound.

In the face of competition, he was granted a patent for the telephone in 1876 and inside a year the first telephone exchange had been built in Connecticut. He soon became a wealthy man as the owner of a third of the shares in the Bell Telephone Company, formed in 1877.

Three years later, Bell was awarded the French Volta Prize for his pioneering work and used the money to conduct experiments in communication, medical research and techniques for teaching speech to the deaf. In this he worked alongside the deaf-blind author Helen Keller.

Bell continued to experiment, particularly in aviation, after moving to Nova Scotia. In 1888, he was made one of the founding members of the National Geographic Society, of which he was president from 1896 to 1904. He died in Nova Scotia in 1922.

Joseph Black
Physician and chemist who discovered latent heat, specific heat and carbon dioxide

Considered one of the founding fathers of chemistry, Black was born in Bordeaux in 1728 but spent his working life in Scotland. Educated at home by his mother, he later studied medicine at Glasgow University and became a laboratory assistant to the chemist Dr William Cullen.

Chemistry became his passion, and

worked on a project to manufacture sodium hydroxide.

Black moved back to Edinburgh in 1766 to become professor of chemistry, and furthered his reputation as both a scientist and a physician. He was called on to give his expert opinion in many areas, and several medical works of the late eighteenth century contain dedications to him.

Black died in 1799 and his obituary was written by the philosopher Adam Ferguson. His impressive grave lies in the churchyard of Greyfriars in Edinburgh. The chemistry buildings of both Glasgow and Edinburgh University are named after him.

Robert the Bruce
King of the Scots who secured independence from England

his meticulous research in the field led to his discovery of carbon dioxide. Black intended to further his carbon dioxide studies but from 1756 became occupied with his professorship of chemistry at the university. Also interested in the science of heat, he clarified the difference between temperature and heat and developed the theory of latent heat.

Collaboration with the inventor and engineer James Watt enabled Black to use steam engines in his lectures on the properties of heat. The two men also

Robert was born in 1274 into an aristocratic family. His grandfather was a claimant to the Scottish throne during a succession dispute between 1290 and 1292, as a result of which Edward I of England came to rule Scotland as a province of England. Bruce supported William Wallace's uprising but after Wallace's defeat became a guardian of

by Edward, he was forced to flee, spending the winter on an island off the Antrim coast.

Returning to Scotland, he waged a successful guerrilla war against the English. At the Battle of Bannockburn in June 1314, Bruce defeated a much larger English army under Edward II, confirming the re-establishment of an independent Scottish monarchy.

Edward refused to give up his claim to Scotland, but in 1320 the Scottish aristocracy, in the Declaration of Arbroath, wrote to the Pope declaring Bruce their rightful monarch. Four years later, Bruce received papal recognition as king of an independent country. The English deposed Edward in 1327 and all claims of superiority over Scotland were finally renounced. Robert died in 1329 and was buried at Dunfermline, with his heart being interred at Melrose Abbey.

Robert Burns

Poet and lyricist, pioneer of the Romantic movement and Scotland's favourite son

Scotland with John Comyn.

In 1306 Bruce, in a quarrel with Comyn, stabbed him in a church in Dumfries and was outlawed by Edward and excommunicated by the Pope. He then proclaimed his right to the throne and was crowned king at Scone. Deposed

Born in Alloway, Ayrshire in 1759, the son of a poor tenant farmer, Burns spent his youth working on the farm, but was well read thanks to his father's employment of a tutor. At fifteen he started to write, and his first poem was an ode to subjects that would recur later in his life: whisky and women.

Having pursued some misadventures with women including Jean Armour, who would become his wife, Burns planned to escape to the West Indies. But his first collection, *Poems – Chiefly in the Scottish Dialect – Kilmarnock Edition*, was published to critical acclaim, and he stayed in Scotland. Moving to Edinburgh, he mingled with artists and writers who marvelled at the 'Ploughman Poet'.

Within a short while he had become a national celebrity, but fame did not bring fortune and he worked as an exciseman to supplement his income. Meanwhile, he was contributing songs to the likes of George Thomson's *Select Collection of Original Scottish Airs*. More than four hundred Burns songs survive to this day.

His last years were devoted to writing poetic masterpieces like *Tam o' Shanter*, *A Red, Red Rose* and *The Lea Rig*. Burns died in Dumfries in 1796, at the age of just thirty-seven. The cause of death was heart disease, which had been exacerbated by the hard manual labour of his youth. More than ten thousand people paid their respects at his funeral.

Thomas Carlyle

Philosopher, sociological writer, historian and teacher

The son of a stonemason, Carlyle was born in Ecclefechan, Dumfriesshire in 1795. Brought up as a strict Calvinist, he learned reading from his mother and arithmetic from his father. He excelled in languages, learning French, Latin, Spanish, Italian and German, and took a keen interest in literature.

Carlyle's father expected him to attend divinity school after the University of Edinburgh; instead, he became a teacher, having lost his Christian faith. Calvinist values, however, remained with him throughout his life.

In 1823 he was asked to write a biographical sketch of the poet Friedrich Schiller for *The London Magazine*. As his writing career progressed he moved to London and developed a close friendship with the philosopher John Stuart Mill. The latter introduced Carlyle to political radicals and suggested he write a book about the French Revolution, which was published in 1837. Charles Dickens used *The French Revolution: A History* as a major source for the events of his novel *A Tale of Two Cities*.

In *Chartism* (1841), Carlyle argued that the immediate answers to poverty and overpopulation were improved education and an expansion of emigration, angering some friends but inspiring social reformers like John Ruskin and William Morris. His other books included *On Heroes, Hero Worship and the Heroic in History* and *Past and Present*.

He later turned against democracy while describing hereditary aristocratic leadership as 'deadening'. He died in Chelsea, London in 1881.

Sir Sean Connery

Oscar-winning actor, producer, the best James Bond ever

Born in Edinburgh in 1930 the son of a lorry driver, Connery grew up in impoverished circumstances. After leaving school he joined the Royal Navy, but was discharged on medical grounds. He then worked as a labourer, a lifeguard and a model for art classes, but made his mark in the 1953 Mr Universe contest.

A job in the chorus of a production of *South Pacific* led to stage appearances and a TV debut in 1956. Connery signed a film contract with MGM in the late 1950s and started the career that was to bring him worldwide fame. Cast as the first cinema James Bond in *Dr No* in 1962, he followed up with three more Bond films in the next five years. He would thereafter appear twice more as Bond.

Connery's roles over the years have been varied, challenging and rewarding. He has worked with directors including Alfred Hitchcock, John Huston and Brian De Palma, and he won the 1987 Oscar for best supporting actor for his performance as the Irish cop Malone in

The Untouchables. He was proclaimed Sexiest Man Alive in 1989.

He received the BAFTA Lifetime Achievement Award in 1990 and the Cecil B DeMille award for an outstanding contribution to entertainment in 1995. He is a Fellow of BAFTA and was knighted in 2000. An avid golfer and Scottish nationalist, Connery retired from acting in 2010.

Billy Connolly
Comedian, musician, actor, perhaps the funniest man who ever drew breath

Connolly, born in Glasgow in 1942, left school early to become a welder in the city's shipyards, also serving in the Territorial Army. As a musician, his career started as half of the Humblebums with Gerry Rafferty. His between-song patter developed into lengthy monologues and led to solo concerts mixing music and talk. The Great Northern Welly Boot Show was received with acclaim.

Already famous in Scotland, Connolly became a nationwide household name after appearing on Michael Parkinson's TV show. His acting career took off in the United States, where he joined the cast of the sitcom *Head of the Class.* From there,

Left: *Billy Connolly – 'If you want to see me in a movie, you have to hurry to the theatre, because I usually die in the first fifteen minutes'*

his character was spun off to lead its own sitcom, *Billy.*

He began to land small roles in films such as *Indecent Proposal* (1993), and he has since acted with some of the biggest names in cinema like Richard Burton, Michael Caine, Mel Gibson and Liam Neeson. The film that won him international recognition as an actor was *Mrs Brown* (1997), in which he played the servant John Brown to Dame Judi Dench's Queen Victoria. He continues to

act, with his role as Wilf Bond in *Quartet* (2012) one of his greatest successes.

Appointed CBE in 2003, Connolly is affectionately known, especially to Scottish audiences, as the Big Yin. He continues to tour his stage show and can be relied on to keep his audiences helpless with laughter.

Sir Alex Ferguson

Footballer, long-serving and perennially successful manager

Ferguson was born in Glasgow in 1941, the son of a plater's helper in the shipyards. He made his debut as a striker for Queen's Park when he was sixteen, scoring in his first match, before moving on to St Johnstone, Dunfermline Athletic, Rangers, Falkirk and Ayr, scoring goals all the while. By the time he retired from playing he had scored 167 times in 327 appearances and had won two Second Division winners' medals.

Ferguson began his management career on a part-time basis with East Stirling in 1974 before moving on to a full-time job at St Mirren, finding immediate success. He joined Aberdeen in 1978, despite being younger than some of the players. He guided the Dons to three Scottish Premier Division titles as well as the UEFA Cup-Winners' Cup and UEFA Super Cup. Even bigger things beckoned.

Joining Manchester United in 1986, Ferguson overcame initial setbacks to win the League Cup in 1991/92 and the Premier League in 1992/93. Since then, his achievements as manager have included twelve further Premier League titles, two UEFA Champions League wins, five FA Cups, four League Cups, one UEFA Cup-Winners' Cup and one FIFA World Club Cup.

A brilliant man-manager who has

influenced and guided the careers of players like David Beckham, Ryan Giggs, Eric Cantona and Ruud van Nistelrooy, Ferguson, the most successful manager of his era, was knighted in 1999.

Alexander Fleming

Biologist, pharmacologist, botanist and the discoverer of penicillin

Fleming was born in Lochfield, Ayrshire in 1881, the son of a farmer. After a two-year scholarship to Kilmarnock Academy, he moved to London at the age of thirteen, later training as a doctor and qualifying with distinction in 1906. He began research at St Mary's Hospital Medical School at the University of London under Sir Almroth Wright, a pioneer in vaccine therapy.

Fleming served in the Army Medical Corps during World War I and was mentioned in dispatches. He returned to St Mary's after the war and gained a reputation as a brilliant, though sometimes untidy, researcher. In 1928, while studying influenza, he noticed that mould had developed on a set of culture dishes being used to grow the staphylococcus bacterium. The mould had created a bacteria-free circle around itself. After

conducting further experiments, Fleming named the active substance penicillin.

Two other scientists, the Australian Howard Florey and Ernst Chain, a refugee from Nazi Germany, went on to develop penicillin further so that it could be produced as an antibiotic drug. At first, supplies were very limited, but by the 1940s the drug was being mass-produced in the United States.

Fleming, who wrote many papers on bacteriology, immunology and chemotherapy, was elected Fellow of the Royal Society in 1943 and was knighted in 1944. In 1945, he shared the Nobel

Above: *Sir Alexander Fleming – son of a farmer, his discovery changed the course of history*

Prize for Medicine with Florey and Chain. He died in London in 1955.

James Keir Hardie
Socialist, first Independent Labour Party MP, first Labour leader

Born in Newhouse, Lanarkshire in 1856, the illegitimate son of a servant, Keir Hardie worked as a baker's delivery boy from the age of eight, being the family's only wage-earner. By the age of eleven he was a coalminer and by seventeen had taught himself to read and write.

Following the setting up of a workers' union at his colliery, he led the first ever strike of Lanarkshire miners in 1881. Keir Hardie was invited to stand as the Independent Labour Party candidate for West Ham in east London in 1892 and duly took his seat in Parliament. Here he advocated women's rights, free education, pensions and Indian self-rule. He was attacked for appearing to criticise the monarchy, and this may have contributed to his defeat in the 1895 election.

Keir Hardie continued to rise through the ranks of union officials and, having served as chairman of the ILP, witnessed the formation of the Labour Representation Committee, which later developed into the Labour Party. He was again elected as an MP, for Merthyr Tydfil, in 1900, and by 1906 he was one of twenty-six Labour MPs.

Elected party leader, he nevertheless resigned in 1908, going on to devote his energies to promoting the party and the cause of equality, particularly women's suffrage. An outspoken pacifist at the start of World War I, Keir Hardie died in Glasgow in 1915.

David Hume
Historian, economist, called 'the most important philosopher ever to write in English'

Hume was born the son of an advocate in an Edinburgh tenement in 1711 and attended university from the age of twelve. After making a philosophical discovery whose nature he never revealed, he set out to spend ten years reading and writing. On the verge of a nervous breakdown, however, he decided to lead a more active life, which would help his learning.

Hume spent four years in the French region of Anjou writing *A Treatise of Human Nature*, completed when he was twenty-six and considered today one of the most important works in western philosophy. In 1751 he published his *Inquiry into the Principles of Morals*, an exposition of the principles of the utilitarian system. *Political Discourses*, which appeared the following year, was followed by *The History of England*, which took fifteen years to complete, contained more than a million words and appeared in six volumes.

Hume went to France in 1763 as secretary to Lord Hertford's embassy. On his return he was appointed to the high office of Under-Secretary of State for the Home Department. He returned to Edinburgh in 1769 'very opulent (for I possessed a revenue of £1,000 a year), healthy, and though somewhat stricken in years, with the prospect of long enjoying my ease, and of seeing the increase of my reputation.' He died in Edinburgh in 1776.

John Knox
Clergyman, firebrand leader of the Protestant Reformation in Scotland

Knox was born in Haddington, East Lothian around 1510. He trained as and became a priest in the Catholic church – a church he would later call 'the synagogue of Satan'. After meeting

the religious reformer George Wishart he preached as a reformer during the siege of St Andrews Castle in 1546/47, spent eighteen months as a galley slave on French warships and became a Protestant preacher in England.

Fleeing to Europe after Mary I restored the Catholic faith in England, Knox met the reformer John Calvin in Geneva. He preached in Scotland in 1555 and was

Above: *David Hume – 'there is more to be learned from each page of David Hume than from the collected philosophical works of Hegel, Herbart and Schleiermacher taken together,' according to Schopenhauer*

Above: *Sir Joseph Lister – micro-organisms and mouthwashes have been named after him*

When Mary, Queen of Scots returned to Scotland in 1561, a Catholic queen in a Protestant country, Knox showed her no pity. Preaching venomous sermons against the queen from the pulpit, he even wrote that God had tried to forewarn the Scots about Mary as 'the sun was not seen to shine two days before nor two days after' her arrival in Edinburgh.

In the years that followed, he would meet Mary face to face in a series of audiences. Knox died in Edinburgh in 1572 after years of illness.

Sir Harry Lauder
Music hall comedian and singer called Scotland's greatest ever ambassador

Henry Lauder was born in Edinburgh in 1870. Having moved to Arbroath with his family, he worked part-time at a flax mill while attending school, and later in coal mines in Lanarkshire. He sang as he worked to help relieve the arduous nature of the work, and his fellow workers encouraged him to sing in local halls. Advised to tour with a concert party, singing comedic songs of Scotland and Ireland, he found success and was able to leave the mines.

In 1905 his success in a pantomime in

burned in effigy by Scottish bishops a year later. In 1558 he published *The First Blast of the Trumpet against the monstrous Regiment of Women*, aimed at Mary, Queen of Scots and Mary I of England. Elizabeth I, the restorer of the Protestant faith, never forgave Knox for this publication.

Glasgow made him a national star and by 1911 he was touring the United States, commanding enormous fees. In 1912 his status as Britain's best-known entertainer was confirmed at a Royal Command Variety Performance.

Lauder toured the world extensively during a forty-year career, and he even had his own train in the US. He was at one point the world's highest-paid performer, making the equivalent of £12,700 a night plus expenses, and was the first British performer to sell a million records.

Performing in Highland dress and signing songs like *Roamin' in the Gloamin'*, *Keep Right on to the End of the Road*, *I Love a Lassie* and *A Wee Deoch-an-Doris* (all of which he wrote himself), he endeared himself to all who saw him. He also starred in three films. He died in Stratheven in 1950, aged 79.

Sir Joseph Lister
Surgeon, pioneer of antiseptic surgery

Although English by birth (Upton, Essex, 1827), Lister married a Scot, spent most of his professional life in Scotland and carried out almost all of his medical research in Scottish hospitals. Born into a Quaker family, he later joined the Scottish Episcopalian Church.

He had decided on a surgical career before he was sixteen and qualified as a doctor as University College, London in 1852. The following year he went to Edinburgh to gain experience under Professor James Syme. In 1860 he became Regius Professor of Surgery at Glasgow University and a year later surgeon at the city's Royal Infirmary. Here he was in charge of a surgical block in which around half of patients died from sepsis following amputations.

Lister theorised that infections were caused by microscopic pollen-like dust. He attempted to protect the operation site by setting up a barrier between the surgeon's hands and instruments, using carbolic acid to soak lint or calico and applying it to the wound. He also switched from using silk, which did not absorb much carbolic acid, to catgut for stitching. Surgical mortality in Lister's ward fell from forty-five to fifteen per cent.

He succeeded Syme in the chair of Clinical Surgery at Edinburgh University in 1869 and became Professor of Surgery at King's College Hospital, London in 1877. He toured Germany to great acclaim but the United States to less. He died in Walmer, Kent in 1912.

David Livingstone
Missionary, explorer, national hero

Livingstone, born in Blantyre in 1813, began working in a cotton mill at the age of ten. He studied medicine and theology in Glasgow from 1836, and decided to become a missionary doctor. In 1841 he was posted to the Kalahari Desert in southern Africa.

His explorations were inspired by his conviction that he should reach peoples, introduce them to Christianity and free them from slavery. In 1849 and 1851 he travelled across the Kalahari, sighting the upper Zambezi River.

In 1852 he began a four-year expedition to find a route from the river to the coast. Livingstone discovered a spectacular waterfall, which he named Victoria Falls, in 1855 and, when he reached the mouth of the Zambezi in 1856, became the first European to cross southern Africa. He returned to Britain and embarked on speaking tours.

By 1858 he was back in Africa, carrying out explorations for the British government. Ordered home, he publicised the horrors of the slave trade and gathered support for another expedition, begun in 1866, to search for the Nile's source and report on slavery. After nothing had been heard from Livingstone for many months, journalist Henry Stanley set out to find him, resulting in the famous meeting near Lake Tangyanika in 1871 at which Stanley asked, 'Dr Livingstone, I presume?'

With new supplies from Stanley, Livingstone continued his expedition. He died in 1873 and was buried in Westminster Abbey.

Mary, Queen of Scots
Queen of Scotland, Queen Consort of France, never Queen of England

Born in Linlithgow Palace in 1542, the only legitimate child of James V of Scotland, Mary became queen soon after on the death of her father. She was betrothed to Henry VIII's son but the Scottish parliament broke the engagement and Henry ordered a series of raids in Scotland known as the Rough Wooing. Mary was sent to France and was brought up at the court of Henry II.

In 1558 she married Henry's son Francis, who became king but died the following year. Returning to Scotland, the Catholic Mary was regarded with suspicion by her Protestant subjects, and ruled with moderation. In 1565 she married her cousin, the Earl of Darnley, but the marriage soured. Darnley was killed by an explosion for which the Earl of Bothwell was a suspect. Three months later, Mary married Bothwell.

The latter was exiled and Mary was forced to abdicate in 1567. Fleeing to England, she sought refuge from her cousin, Elizabeth I. But Mary, who had a strong claim to the English throne, posed a threat to Elizabeth, who had her imprisoned. Over the next nineteen years, Mary became the focus of numerous plots to assassinate Elizabeth and put her on the throne.

Mary, tried and condemned to death in 1586, was eventually executed on 8 February 1587. Her son James went on to succeed Elizabeth in 1603.

John McAdam
Engineer, road builder, inventor of macadam

Born in Ayr in 1756, McAdam was the second son of the Baron of Waterhead. He moved to New York in 1770, made a fortune as a merchant and returned to Scotland in 1783, buying an estate in Ayrshire. A trustee of the Ayrshire Turnpike from 1783, he became increasingly involved in road construction.

In 1802 he moved to Bristol and became general surveyor for the city's Corporation. He began to put forward his ideas for road construction and, in treatises written in 1816 and 1819, argued that roads needed to be raised above the surrounding ground and constructed from layered stones and

Above: *Mary, Queen of Scots – few people of any era have led such an eventful, and finally tragic, life*

gravel in a systematic manner.

Appointed surveyor to the Bristol Turnpike Trust in 1816, McAdam decided to remake roads under his care with crushed stone bound with gravel on a firm base of large stones. A camber ensured rainwater drained off the road rather than damage the foundations.

The method, dubbed macadamisation or macadam, spread rapidly across the world. The first macadam road in North America was completed in the 1830s and most main roads in Europe had been subject to McAdam's process by the end of the nineteenth century.

Professional jealousy ensured that an expenses grant to McAdam from parliament was cut from £5,000 to £2,000. His work had revealed the extent of corruption and abuse of road tolls by turnpike trusts. McAdam died in Moffat, Dumfriesshire in 1836, at the age of eighty.

James Nasmyth
Engineer, inventor of the steam hammer

Born in Edinburgh in 1808, Nasmyth was encouraged by his father to join him in his hobby of mechanics. At school he met the son of an iron founder and spent much time at the foundry learning to work and turn in wood, brass, iron and steel.

At the age of seventeen he made his first steam engine and a few years later a complete steam carriage. The accomplishment increased his desire to become a mechanical engineer. In 1829 he was appointed private workman to Henry Maudslay, machine tool innovator, in London and, on returning to Edinburgh, set up his own business, the Bridgewater Foundry, in 1836.

Nasmyth invented the screw ladle for moving molten metal and soon began to receive orders from newly opened railways. He was also asked to make machine tools of unusual size and power for the construction of paddle-ship engines. He developed an idea for the steam hammer and patented it in 1842. Before long, Nasmyth hammers were to be found in workshops all over the country.

He applied the steam hammer principle to a piledriving machine he invented in 1843, and among his other inventions were a means of transmitting rotary motion by means of a flexible shaft made of coiled wire, a machine for cutting key grooves, self-adjusting bearings, a steam ram and a hydraulic press.

Nasmyth, arguably the last of the early machine tool pioneers, died in Kent in 1890.

Mungo Park
Explorer, first westerner to find the central part of the Niger River

Park was born in 1771 at Foulshiels in the Borders and educated at the Grammar School in nearby Selkirk. He became an apprentice surgeon and went on to study medicine at the University of Edinburgh before moving to London and securing a position as Assistant Surgeon on an East India Company ship in 1792.

In this role, he was able to make scientific observations and collect examples of flora and fauna during a trip to Sumatra. On his return in 1794, he reported several new species in a paper he gave to the Linnaean Society in London. On the recommendation of the scientist Sir Joseph Banks, Park was commissioned by the African Association to explore the course of the River Niger.

During two expeditions to West Africa, in 1795 and 1805, he became the first man to map large areas of the interior. His first expedition determined that the

river flowed from west to east, and his diary was published in 1799 as *Travels in the Interior of Africa*. Park set out on the second expedition intending to find the outflow of the Niger, but after following the river's course for some distance he was killed by local people near Boussa.

News of his death took several years to be confirmed, but his papers were eventually recovered and published in 1815 as *The Journal of a Mission to the Interior of Africa*.

Above: *Mungo Park – it took several years for news of his death to be confirmed*

Right: *Adam Smith – often described as the father of modern economics*

JK Rowling
Writer of the best-selling book series in history

Joanne Rowling was born in 1965 in Gloucestershire, the daughter of a half-Scottish mother. She gained a French and Classics degree at Exeter University, and thereafter worked as a researcher at Amnesty International in London, among other jobs. She started writing the Harry Potter series during a delayed train journey, and over the next five years outlined the plots for each book and began writing the first novel.

After teaching English in Portugal, Rowling returned to live in Edinburgh, a city that has influenced her deeply, and completed Harry Potter & The Philosopher's Stone. It was published in 1997, and the second novel, Harry Potter & the Chamber of Secrets, appeared the following year. By the time The Prisoner of Azkaban was published in 1999 the series was a worldwide publishing phenomenon.

The fourth book, *Harry Potter & the Goblet of Fire*, was published in 2000 with a UK record first print-run of a million copies, and broke the record for the number of books sold on the first day of publication. The series continued with *The Order of the Phoenix* and *The Half-Blood Prince*, and was completed with the publication of *Harry Potter & the Deathly Hallows* in 2007.

Also the author of an adult novel, *The Casual Vacancy* (2012), Rowling was appointed OBE for her services to children's literature and has received honours including France's Légion d'Honneur.

Adam Smith
Political economist, philosopher, author of the first modern work of economics

Smith was born in Kirkcaldy, Fife in 1723 to a father who was a lawyer and civil servant. From the age of fourteen he studied moral philosophy at Glasgow and Oxford Universities and returned to Kirkcaldy in 1746. Two years later, he was asked to give a series of lectures in Edinburgh that served to establish his reputation.

He was appointed Professor of Logic at Glasgow University in 1751 and a year later became Professor of Moral Philosophy. He was part of an intellectual circle that included David Hume, John Home, Lord Hailes and William Robertson. In 1764, while travelling in Europe as tutor to the future Duke of Buccleuch, Smith met a number of leading intellectuals including Voltaire, Jean-Jacques Rousseau and François Quesnay.

He moved to London in 1776 and published a volume that he intended to be the first part of a complete theory of society, covering theology, ethics, politics and law. *An Inquiry into the Nature and Causes of the Wealth of Nations* was the first major work of political economy. Smith argued strongly against the regulation of commerce and trade, insisting that setting people free to better themselves would produce economic prosperity for all.

He was appointed commissioner of customs in Edinburgh in 1778 and in 1783 became a founding member of the Royal Society of Edinburgh. He died in the city in 1790.

Robert Louis Stevenson
Novelist, poet, travel writer and author of Treasure Island

The son of a lighthouse engineer, Stevenson was born in 1850 in Edinburgh. He suffered breathing problems that later developed into tuberculosis, which left him weak and sickly for most of his life.

By the time he entered Edinburgh University to study engineering, at the age of sixteen, he had begun to write. He developed a bohemian existence, complete with long hair, and when he was twenty-one he declared his intention of becoming a writer, an aim his father opposed strongly. Agreeing to study law as a compromise, he was admitted to the Scottish bar in 1875 but began to travel widely.

His first book, *An Inland Voyage* (1878), related his experiences during a canoe trip on Belgian and French canals. In America he stayed in an abandoned

mining camp, a stay later recounted in *The Silverado Squatters* (1883). The following years in Switzerland and France proved productive, but it was with the publication of *Treasure Island* in 1881 that Stevenson rose to prominence. *Kidnapped* and *David Balfour* followed, and in *The Strange Case of Dr Jekyll and Mr Hyde* (1886) he dealt with the nature of evil in man, to popular acclaim.

In 1889, Stevenson settled on the Samoan island of Upolu, becoming known as the Teller of Tales, and his observations on Samoan life were published in *A Footnote to History* (1892) and *In the South Seas* (1896). He died in Samoa in 1894.

William Wallace

Leader of a rebellion, victor at Stirling Bridge, national hero

Wallace was born into the gentry in the 1270s in Elderslie, Renfrewshire, but little is known about his early life. In 1297, following the imposition of English administration in Scotland, he attacked the town of Lanark and killed the English sheriff.

Men flocked to Wallace's side and he began to drive the English out of

Fife and Perthshire. In September 1297 he defeated a much larger English force at the Battle of Stirling Bridge, and this and subsequent victories weakened the English grip on Scotland. After launching raids into England, he was knighted and appointed guardian of the kingdom.

The English rallied and marched north. Wallace, avoiding confrontation, retreated and forced the enemy to march

Above: *William Wallace – national hero*
Far Left: *RL Stevenson – much translated author*

further and further into Scotland. The armies met in 1298 near Falkirk and the Scots were defeated, but Wallace escaped. Resigning the guardianship, he went to France to seek support and returned in 1303. Peace terms had been agreed during his absence, and the English king Edward I offered a large sum of money to anyone who killed or captured Wallace.

He was captured in or near Glasgow in 1305 and taken to London, where he was tried for treason. This he denied, saying he had never sworn allegiance to an English king. Nevertheless, Wallace was hanged, drawn and quartered; his head was placed on London Bridge and his limbs were displayed in Newcastle, Berwick, Stirling and Perth.

James Watt
Mechanical engineer, inventor, pioneer of steam engine technology

The son of a wealthy shipwright, Watt was born in Greenock in 1736. He worked initially as a maker of mathematical instruments, but soon became interested in steam engines, the first of which had been patented in 1698. By the time of Watt's birth, Newcomen engines were pumping water from mines all over the country.

Given a model Newcomen engine in around 1764, he soon realised that it was hopelessly inefficient and set to work to improve the design. He designed a separate condensing chamber that prevented the Newcomen engine's enormous losses of steam; his first patent, in 1769, covered this device and other improvements.

In 1775, Watt started to manufacture steam engines with his partner, Matthew Boulton, in Birmingham, and Boulton & Watt became the most important engineering firm in the country. To begin with, demand came from Cornish mine owners, but it soon extended to the owners of paper, flour, cotton and iron mills, distilleries, canals and waterworks. Watt and Boulton were elected Fellows of the Royal Society in 1785.

By 1790, when he retired to devote himself to research work, Watt was a wealthy man. He patented several other important inventions, including the rotary engine, the double-action engine and the steam indicator, which records steam pressure inside an engine. He died in 1819. A unit of measurement of electrical and mechanical power, the watt, is named in his honour.

Left: *James Watt –
his improvements
in steam engine
technology drove
the Industrial
Revolution*

Tim'rous Beasties

TIM'ROUS BEASTIES

Far Right: *The red squirrel – Scotland is one of its few remaining strongholds in the British Isles*

Scotland, with its diverse range of habitats and (with a few local exceptions) generally temperate climate, is a nature lover's delight. From snow-peaked mountains to rushing rivers, from desolate moorlands to forests of pines, the landscape supports a vast array of animal life. Scots are justly proud of their fauna, from the mighty red deer to the tiniest freshwater mussel, and Scottish wildlife is one of the greatest attractions drawing visitors from all corners of the world.

For some, it's all summed up by one of the best-known paintings to have started life on an artist's easel in Scotland. The English painter Sir Edwin Landseer had made a number of minutely observed studies of red deer on his many trips to the Highlands before he produced *The Monarch of the Glen* in 1851. His painting captures a magnificent stag with branching antlers in an imperious pose against a craggy mountain backdrop, and has enchanted generations of art lovers and wildlife lovers alike.

The red deer is indeed emblematic of Scotland, even though the species inhabits many parts of the world. The fourth largest deer species in existence, behind the moose, the elk and the sambar deer, it is mainly to be found on the country's moors and hillsides. Scotland's red deer population is around the 300,000 mark – double the number estimated in 1965 – although it's feared that interbreeding with sika deer, which

Above: *The unmistakable male capercaillie – largest member of the grouse family*

echo with the testosterone-fuelled bellowing of the stags.

Red deer are not the only even-toed ungulates to be seen in Scotland. Herds of roe deer are to be found on lower-lying land, feral goats and sheep flourish in some upland and coastal areas, and even semi-domesticated reindeer – once one of Scotland's indigenous species – can be seen in the Cairngorms National Park.

A very different type of mammal, the Scottish wildcat, is another species that faces a threat through its habit of interbreeding: it's not averse to mating with domestic and feral cats. Of all Scotland's mammals the wildcat is the most difficult to catch a glimpse of, for it's a secretive kind of beast and there are very few left, but you can sometimes find its droppings, typically containing bone and feather fragments.

Sadly, the wildcat is in real danger of extinction, with some estimates putting the population as low as thirty-five. One of its favourite food sources, the rabbit, has been badly affected by outbreaks of myxomatosis, with the inevitable serious consequences for the wildcat.

Another hard-to-spot carnivore is the pine marten but, unlike the wildcat, your chances of seeing one are increasing. This

have escaped into the wild following their introduction to parklands, could threaten efforts to conserve the species. Red deer stags and hinds (females) live in separate herds for much of the year, but when they come together for the autumn rut (mating season), the hills beautiful member of the weasel family, once shot for its fur, has benefited from the spread of pine plantations and is sometimes bold enough to enter gardens in search of food. The pine marten is a nocturnal animal whose natural habitat is wooded areas, for it's at home climbing and exploring trees. It eats a wide variety of food, including other mammals, birds and their eggs, frogs and berries. Some people tempt martens into their gardens with fruity jams and even peanut butter.

Scotland is one of an increasingly small number of places in the British Isles where you're likely to come across a red squirrel rather than the grey species that has driven it out from much of the UK. The delightful red squirrel's distinctive russet fur and tufted ears can be seen across large areas of Dumfries and Galloway and the Central Highlands, and in all Scotland can claim three-quarters of the UK's population. Nevertheless, the larger grey squirrel still represents a threat to its smaller cousin, and conservation experts are busy working out ways of protecting *Sciurus vulgaris*. One way may be to encourage the proliferation of pine martens, which seem to prefer the taste of grey squirrels to that of reds.

The mountain hare, typically Scottish but also found from Scandinavia to Siberia, goes by many names: the tundra hare, blue hare, snow hare, alpine hare, white hare, even variable hare. As you might guess, it's a species that is adapted to mountainous habitats. To be found in Scottish uplands and on many islands, its party trick is turning its brown coat white in winter, partly for means of camouflage and partly for the white fur's superior heat-retaining properties – it's effectively just a winter coat. The mountain hare is Scotland's only native member of the hare family, although the brown hare can also be found.

The Orkney vole is something of a puzzle for naturalists. Its closest relatives are to be found at the other end of Europe in the Balkan states and, in Scotland, it can only be found on five Orkney islands: Mainland, Rousay, Sanday, South Ronaldsay and Westray. This animal is otherwise known as the common vole, but it's far from common in the UK: it occurs nowhere else in the British Isles. How it got to Scotland is anyone's guess, but work by scientists points to this fascinating creature being introduced to Orkney by humans in Neolithic times.

The Scottish islands pose another interesting question in the field of small, mouse-like mammals: how come St Kilda field mice are so big? These animals, which can be found only in the St Kilda archipelago of the Outer Hebrides, are twice the size and weight of field mice on the mainland, and have longer fur and tails. The last permanent human settlements in St Kilda were evacuated in 1930, and researchers feel that the field mice took advantage of the absence of man to colonise the buildings that were left behind. It's thought the lack of predators and competition allowed the little beasts to grow larger, which in turn permitted them to cope better with the challenging climate.

One mammal making a comeback in Scotland is the European beaver, which was last seen in the country in the fifteenth century. Eleven beavers from Norway were introduced in the Knapdale area of Argyll in 2009, and they were followed by further introductions. This could be good news for other Scottish fauna, because beaver populations have been found to benefit bats, salmon and trout.

Scottish mammals are not confined to land, of course: two seal species – the grey seal and the common or harbour seal – are found in Scottish waters. The grey seal population is in fact huge – around 120,000 adults, more than a third of the entire world population – while there are around 30,000 common seals, about a third of the European total. Most grey seals frequent the country's rocky western coast while the slightly smaller common seal is more widespread.

Whales, dolphins and porpoises are no strangers to Scottish waters, and the colony of bottlenose dolphins in the Moray Firth is especially well known. Another familiar cetacean is the harbour porpoise, which loves shallow waters and is to be found in good numbers around the Hebrides and Northern Isles. Among whales seen around the coasts of Scotland are the ocean's supreme predator, the orca, and the minke whale.

If there is a challenger to the red deer for the title of Scotland's most iconic animal, it's perhaps the golden eagle. Once this huge, magnificent bird ranged over much of upland Britain, but thanks to idiotic persecution and changes in habitat, it's now confined to the wildest parts of the Scottish Highlands and islands. The golden eagle is Britain's second largest bird of prey with a wingspan of around two metres, and the larger females can reach a weight of about five kilos. The last population survey, in 2003, counted

442 pairs – a figure that has stayed fairly constant for some time.

Golden eagles can be seen soaring over open moorlands and mountains, often in search of prey including hares, rabbits, ptarmigan, grouse and even deer and calves. They also feed on carrion. Their territories are often vast and can contain two nest sites, which they use alternately.

The only British bird of prey larger than the golden eagle is the white-tailed eagle. This enormous bird was driven into extinction in Britain in the early twentieth century, having bred purely on the Scottish west coast, but it's now also being reintroduced on the eastern seaboard. Haliaeetus albicilla, to give it its Latin name, can be differentiated from the golden eagle by its wedge-shaped tail (coloured white in adults) and pale head

Above *Bottlenose dolphin with young – those in the Moray Firth are the world's most northerly residents of their species*

Above: *Red deer – one of Scotland's emblematic animals*

and neck. You may be lucky enough to spot one over the cliffs or mountains of the west coast, on the lookout for fish or birds.

Another bird of prey that has a taste for fish is of course the osprey – and there's no more rewarding sight in the natural world than that of an osprey swooping majestically to snatch a struggling fish from the waters of a loch. This spectacular bird is much easier to spot than the white-

tailed eagle thanks to the 'nestcams' that follow its activities at nesting sites in Speyside and Perth. Ospreys return each year to Scotland and other parts of Britain from their wintering sites in West Africa. They are black and white birds that can sometimes be mistaken for seagulls from a distance, but there's no mistaking them close up. If you're in Scotland between April and August, it's worth going out of your way to the visitor centre at Loch of the Lowes, north of Perth, to watch ospreys fishing at close quarters.

Another Scottish bird that puts on a spectacular display is the capercaillie – but this show is nothing to do with feeding. The male of the largest member of the grouse family puts on an extravagant display in its courtship area (known as a lek), pointing its wings downwards, flaring its tails and jutting its 'beard'. All the while, it gives vent to an extraordinary series of sounds: wheezes, gurgles and cork-popping noises. Fights between rival males are not unknown, and they can even end in death. The male capercaillie is a handsome bird with brown wings and white patches on the shoulders, blue head, neck and breast and red rings round the eyes. They're found in the pinewoods of northern Scotland but, sad to say, they're in decline and in danger of extinction.

Populations of the red grouse and black grouse are also on the wane, but the good news is that habitat management is helping to reverse the trend in some places. The black grouse is to be found in most areas of Scotland; look for them all year round on farmland or moorland with trees nearby. Males – which, like the capercaillie, display on leks in the breeding season – are all black with red wattles above the eyes, and have lyre-shaped tails which they fan out when displaying. Sadly, females are much drabber, brownish creatures. There's more equality of the sexes in the red grouse, which is a reddish-brown colour all over except for the male's red eye-patches. Many a walker on upland moors has been alarmed as one startled grouse after another bursts out of the heather with noisy, frantic wingbeats.

The ptarmigan is another bird of the grouse family to be found in Scotland, but only in the Arctic-like areas of the highest mountains. It's notable for the fact that it turns white in winter except for its tail and eye-patch.

Let's finish this chapter on Scotland's glorious wildlife with a look at Britain's only endemic bird – that's to say it's found in the UK and nowhere else in the world: the Scottish crossbill. This is a thickset little finch that inhabits the pine forests of the Highlands, where it uses its distinctive crossed beak to extract pine seeds. It has brown, white, red, orange and grey plumage, but the truth is it's difficult to tell the Scottish crossbill from other members of its family. Never mind: it's Scotland's, and Scotland's alone.

Flower of Scotland

With its variety of climates and range of habitats, the country can boast a huge array of plant species to delight the visitor, but there are a few that speak the word 'Scotland' more clearly than any guidebook ever could. They extend from the tiniest flower of Scotland to the high and the mighty.

The sight of acres of moorland covered with blooming heather have always sent poets scrabbling for their pens and visitors for their cameras. Heather is as expressive of Scotland as its national emblem, the thistle. As the poet G Bennett put it:

No foreign strand, no classic land,
Earth's fairest scenes together,

Can win our praise like yonder braes,
And fragrant hills of purple Heather.

Otherwise known as ling, heather belongs to the plant family of ericaceae and, although it's most associated with Scotland, can be found on heathland and moorland across Europe. It's thought there are five million acres of this beautiful, hardy shrub across the country, and heathery carpets usually range from the classic purple to a more delicate shade of lilac. White heather also grows wild but it's much less common (and a traditional sign of good luck) and even gold, red and silver-grey blooms can sometimes be found.

Heather usually blooms twice in

Above: *Heather – five million Scottish acres are carpeted with this lovely shrub*

Scotland, at either end of the summer, but the best time to see it is often between late July and early September.

It's somehow appropriate that a plant most often regarded as a weed – the thistle – should become a national emblem of a country in which the humblest men and women have often risen to prominence. There is actually some dispute as to which variety of thistle starred in the legendary story that led to it becoming Scotland's national flower (see final chapter). The Cotton Thistle is most often cited as the species in question, although it's thought not to have existed in Scotland at the time of the legend. The most likely contender is the Spear Thistle, a widespread native species, but arguments have been made in favour of the Dwarf Thistle, the Musk Thistle and the wonderfully named Melancholy Thistle.

Apart from the legend, there's another explanation for why Scots should exhibit so much pride in the thistle: behind its soft exterior beauty lies a prickly defence and a stubborn tenacity – traits that could be said to mirror the national character, if such a thing exists. Certainly, any gardener who has tried to rid his land of thistles knows only too well that any time he thinks he's succeeded, up springs another plant.

There are many other plant species that are emblematic of Scotland, and some of them are a good deal larger than the thistle and the heather. One of these is the Scots Pine, the only pine that is native to Britain

Above: *Scots pine – a keystone species in the Scottish ecosystem, forming a backbone on which many other species depend*

from putting down roots. Sadly, what the weather cannot do, man can – the massive deforestation that has taken place over the centuries in Scotland means that just one per cent of what used to make up the ancient Caledonian forests still remains. Today, projects are under way in places such as Glen Affric, to the west of Loch Ness, to protect and restore parts of the old forests.

There's no denying it: the adult Scots pine is a peculiar-looking tree. With its uneven, twisted branches and patches of foliage, it seems to have a permanent weather-beaten look, a far cry from the more evenly spaced branches and conical shape of its youth. As it grows older, the tree casts off its lower branches and its crown flattens out, and it can eventually reach a height of over thirty metres.

The rowan, often known as the mountain ash, is another of Scotland's iconic trees, and with good reason. It grows at a higher altitude than any other tree in the country, and can be found at altitudes of over a thousand metres in parts of the Highlands, although at these elevations it does little more than survive as a small sapling. The rowan is also well known for growing in inaccessible places like the steep banks of streams, on cliffs

despite the huge conifer plantations to be found in Scotland and elsewhere.

Sometimes called the country's national tree, the Scots pine is in fact found as far south as Spain, as far north as Lapland and as far east as Siberia. It's suited to the Highlands of Scotland, whose tough conditions do nothing to deter it and on top of boulders. It's not that it chooses these places, rather that they are sometimes the only locations where the tree is out of the reach of sheep and deer that are fond of its foliage.

A member of the rose family, the rowan is a small tree that reaches a height of ten to fifteen metres. Its bright red berries, which are rich in vitamin C, put on a glorious show in August and early September, attracting the birds that help its propagation by spreading the seeds far and wide. The rowan – the name comes from the Gaelic words for 'red one' – has had a long association with the folklore of Scotland, having been planted in the graveyards of long ago to keep the dead in their graves. It was also thought to be able to protect people and livestock from witches.

No such supernatural powers are attributed to two plant species that can be found nowhere else in the world but in the very north of Scotland: the Scottish Primrose and the Shetland Mouse-Ear.

The first is a lovely little plant with dark purple flowers that grows on moist but well-drained, grazed grasslands in Caithness, Sutherland and Orkney. The Scottish Primrose can be seen, if you're lucky, from May to July, and to improve your chances you might head for Hill of

Above: *The thistle – another emblematic Scottish species*

White Hamars on Stromness, Orkney. The Shetland Mouse-Ear, in contrast, is only found on two hills on Unst in Shetland. Its flowers, to be seen in June and July, are white with grey veins, and it has purplish, fleshy leaves. These little survivors are just two more of Scotland's unique offerings.

Must-see Marvels

No short-term visitor to Scotland ever has enough time to explore all of the wonders the country has to offer. That's hardly surprising; perhaps even a lifetime is not long enough. But in this chapter we will look in some detail at just a tiny fraction of the marvels it would be foolish to leave Scotland without experiencing. There are many, many more.

Edinburgh's Old Town is a brilliant example of the preservation of a medieval street plan and buildings of the Reformation era. At one end sits Edinburgh Castle; away from it leads the main artery, the High Street or Royal Mile. Off this thoroughfare sprout minor streets called closes or wynds. Large squares mark the location of markets or surround public buildings such as St Giles' Cathedral and the Law Courts. Places of interest include the Royal Museum of Scotland, the Surgeons' Hall and the Royal Festival Theatre.

Edinburgh's topography was created aeons ago when glaciers pushed soft soil aside but were split by crags of volcanic rock. The hilltop crag was the earliest part of the city to be developed, and it eventually became the Edinburgh Castle we see today. The rest of the city grew down the tail of land from the Castle Rock.

The Old Town's space restrictions led to it becoming home to early high-

rise buildings: multistorey dwellings were the norm from the 1500s. Many buildings were destroyed in the Great Fire of 1824 but were rebuilt on the original foundations. This led to changes in the ground level and the creation of fascinating passages and vaults under the Old Town.

To find out about the life of Scotland's national bard Robert Burns, travel to Ayrshire and see where he was born. The Robert Burns Birthplace Museum in Alloway houses the world's most important Burns collection, including his writing set, pistols and even a cast of his skull. The museum is set in ten acres of countryside that includes buildings and landmarks connected to the poet's life, including Burns Cottage (where he was born in 1759), the Brig O' Doon (from his poem *Tam O' Shanter*) and the Burns Monument.

To follow in Burns' footsteps as he moved to the Dumfries & Galloway region, visit his former home, Ellisland Farm, now a museum. Here you can see some of his original writings and possessions. The poet's final home, Robert Burns House in Dumfries, houses the famous Kilmarnock and Edinburgh editions of his work and the study in which he wrote. Around the corner you can enjoy a drink at the Globe Inn, Burns' local 'howff'. Here you can see his chair, but beware – if you sit on it you

Above: *Glasgow Science Centre – presents science and technology in inspiring ways*

hundred square miles, stretching from rolling hills and moorland in the west through gentler valleys to rich agricultural plains in the east and the rocky Berwickshire coastline with secluded coves and picturesque fishing villages.

Through it all, tracing a glittering course from the hills to the sea, runs the River Tweed, fed by many tributaries and providing some of Scotland's best fishing. If your preference is semi-urban life, you should schedule a visit to one of the region's towns: perhaps Melrose, with its ruined twelfth century abbey; Coldstream, once a rival to Gretna for runaway marriages; Galashiels, a former textiles stronghold; Jedburgh, where David I founded the red sandstone abbey; or Selkirk, where Sir Walter Scott served as sheriff for thirty-three years.

The region's castles, abbeys, stately homes and museums illustrate its often bloody history. It's a history that is commemorated in the Common Ridings (see following chapter) and other local festivals, creating colourful pageants enjoyed by visitors and native Borderers alike. As this is a region famed for its textiles, you may want to buy tweeds, tartans and knitwear from one of the many mills and shops.

have either to recite a line from one of his poems or stand a round of drinks.

The gorgeous countryside and welcoming towns and villages of the Scottish Borders cover about eighteen

Sitting on the south bank of the River Clyde, Glasgow Science Centre presents science and technology in inspiring ways to visitors of all ages. Familiar for its stunning, titanium-clad crescent shape and its free-standing tower, the centre has two acres of interactive exhibits, workshops, shows, activities, a planetarium and an IMAX cinema.

The Centre is home to hundreds of interactive exhibits located on the three floors of its Science Mall. Exhibits allow visitors to 'be creative, be innovative' or question their values in Science in the Dock; while younger visitors may take the helm of a ship on the Big Explorer and journey down the rabbit hole into Alice's Wonderland. You can explore the underwater universe, discover the marine reptiles that ruled the ancient seas, travel into space, control objects with the power of your mind or build a rollercoaster.

The IMAX cinema offers 3D effects and Scotland's biggest screen, and the wonders of the night sky can be explored in the Planetarium, which features seven thousand twinkling stars. At 127 metres high, Glasgow Tower is Scotland's tallest free-standing building. It's also the tallest tower in the world in which the whole structure can be rotated 360 degrees.

Kelvingrove Art Gallery and Museum, on Argyle Street in Glasgow's West End, is one of Scotland's most popular free attractions. It features twenty-two themed galleries displaying the extraordinary number of eight thousand objects.

The extensive, internationally significant collections at Kelvingrove include paintings and sculptures, silver and ceramics, European armour, weapons and firearms (one of the world's finest collections), clothing and furniture. The natural history of Scotland is treated in depth and there are displays of relics from the country's history and prehistory. Sir Roger the Asian elephant is another big museum attraction, and there is even a Spitfire aircraft hanging from the ceiling of the west court.

Kelvingrove's art collection includes many outstanding European works including pieces from the Old Masters, French Impressionists, the Dutch Renaissance, Scottish Colourists and exponents of the Glasgow School. The most famous painting on display is the Salvador Dali masterpiece *Christ of St John of the Cross*. Another notable paintings include *Portrait of the Art Dealer Alexander Reid* by Vincent van Gogh and *A Man in Armour* by Rembrandt.

The refurbished building – reopened in 2006 after a three-year refurbishment – is an attraction in its own right and Kelvingrove's displays have been designed with children in mind.

Measuring seventy-one square kilometres and lying just thirty kilometres north-west of Glasgow, enchanting Loch Lomond is Britain's largest inland expanse of water. The loch was formed during the last ice age by the action of glaciers, and it was later at the junction of three ancient kingdoms: Strathclyde, Dalriada and Pictland.

The loch crosses the Highland fault line, which makes for more rugged terrain as you move from south to north. The highest mountain in the area, Ben Lomond, sits on the eastern shore and the loch plays host to thirty-seven islands, some of which made perfect retreats for early Christians. One of them, Inchmurrin, is the largest freshwater island in Britain.

On the western shore of the loch is Balloch, the place to head to for boat trips. The most picturesque of the villages here is Luss, but also on the western side are the villages of Arden, Tarbet and Ardlui. On the eastern side lies the scenic West Highland railway, and here can be found the start of the 'tourist route' up Ben Lomond. Sitting behind the village of Balmaha is Conic Hill, a mound that marks the start of the Highlands and a starting point for boat excursions.

To visit the visually astonishing Falkirk Wheel, a wonder of modern Scotland, head for the environs of Falkirk, about twenty miles from both Glasgow and Edinburgh. This amazing feat of engineering is the world's only rotating boat lift, used to connect the Forth & Clyde and Union canals, and is a must-not-miss sight.

Designed to replace a series of lock gates built in the nineteenth century, the Wheel is the showpiece of a millennium project through which coast-to-coast navigation of the canals was re-established after over forty years. The Forth & Clyde canal, opened in 1773, extended from Grangemouth on the River Forth to Bowling on the Clyde; the Edinburgh & Glasgow Union canal, operating from Edinburgh to Falkirk, was opened in 1822; a series of locks connected the two canals at Port Downie in Camelon. The locks were demolished years ago; then, in 2002, along came the Wheel.

Costing £17.5 million to build, it's thirty-five metres tall. Its construction necessitated the use of 1,200 tonnes of steel, more than fourteen thousand bolts and forty-five thousand bolt holes. The gondolas hold half a million litres of water, but the Wheel only uses 1.5 KWh of energy to turn – the same amount as it takes to boil eight household kettles.

Beating famous lines like the Trans-Siberian and Peru's Cuzco to Machu Picchu to the title of the world's top rail journey, the West Highland Line is the most beautifully scenic railway line in Britain.

Linking the west coast ports of Mallaig and Oban to Glasgow, the railway leaves the big city and skirts the Firth of Clyde before climbing above Loch Lomond, continuing through Glen Falloch and Strath Fillan and crossing the desolately beautiful Rannoch Moor. At Corrour the line descends through the heart of the Highlands past Loch Treig, before following Glen Spean to the resort town of Fort William. After running alongside Loch Eil, the line climbs to Glenfinnan, crossing the curved viaduct featured in the Harry Potter films.

From Lochailort onwards there are glimpses of Scotland's dramatic north-

Above: *The Falkirk Wheel – the world's only rotating boat lift*

Above: *Bowmore distillery, Islay – one of Scotland's oldest, said to have been established in 1779.*

A short drive from Oban, on the shores of Loch Awe, is one of the most awe-inspiring sights you will ever see, a concealed wonder of the Highlands: a power station hidden deep within the mountain of Ben Cruachan. The 'Hollow Mountain Power Station' is buried a kilometre below the ground.

A short coach journey transports visitors into the mountain, at the centre of which lies a vast cavern high enough to house the Tower of London. You will be taken up the visitors' walkway, past sub-tropical plants that grow strongly thanks to the warm, humid conditions, and then on to the viewing gallery. From here you can see the generating hall housing the four turbine generators that are used to produce electricity from water. The remarkable experience continues above ground in a visitor centre.

Cruachan power station, constructed between 1959 and 1965, was the world's first reversible pump storage hydroelectric system. It is capable of generating 440 MW of electricity and can go from standby to full production in two minutes. It can operate for twenty-two hours before the supply of water in the top reservoir (360 metres above Loch Awe) is exhausted. And all this goes on hidden from view.

western coastline, and the islands of Eigg, Muck and Rum can be seen before the train terminates at the picturesque fishing village of Mallaig. In the summer you travel between Fort William and Mallaig by *The Jacobite* steam train. And at Crianlarich there's a branch line to the port of Oban, with its ferry connections to outlying islands.

A visit to a Scotch whisky distillery is an indispensable part of any visit to Scotland. Many distilleries offer visitors the chance to witness the distilling and maturing process for themselves, and it's difficult to choose just one. But for the purposes of this chapter, choose one we must, and the Bowmore Distillery offers an excuse for a visit to the lovely island of Islay.

This is one of Scotland's oldest distilleries, having stood on the shores of Loch Indaal since 1779. Its proximity to the sea plays a major role in determining the character of Bowmore Islay Single Malt, as does a strict adherence to traditional production methods. Bowmore is one of a dwindling number of distilleries that produce their own floor-malted barley, and the water used comes from the Laggan River. Having spent two thousand years percolating through rock in the hills above, the water gathers the flavour of peat – the same stuff that fires the distillery's malt-drying kiln.

What's produced spends nearly all of its life resting quietly in damp cellars below sea level, where Spanish and American oak casks impart rich, mellow flavours to the maturing whisky. After all those years, it's surely time for a dram.

Above: *Ben Nevis – its summit, the collapsed dome of a volcano, features the ruins of an observatory*

It's almost a certainty that you have been asking yourself 'When are we going to hear about Ben Nevis?' The answer is 'now'. Britain's loftiest mountain, at 1,344 metres (4,406 feet) is impossible to ignore for long. Dominating the landscape of Fort William, the 'Ben', as it's known to local people, sits majestically at the head of Loch Linnhe, its presence obvious from all corners of the town and some parts of Lochaber. Some say the mountain has almost a paternal presence.

The mountain's Gaelic name, Beinn Nibheis, has been linked with words meaning poisonous or terrible, implying a fairly ominous character. Ben Nevis, although not as high as Alpine mountains, is positioned on a more northerly latitude and the climate can be considered similar to Arctic regions. While there may be a welcoming sea breeze on the shores of Loch Linnhe, twenty to thirty knots of chilling wind may be evident on the summit of the Ben.

The mountain attracts around 100,000 ascents a year, with three-quarters of the climbers and walkers using the Pony Path from Glen Nevis. Many find weather conditions changing within minutes – usually for the worse – as they work their way up, so common sense is called for.

From the heights of Ben Nevis, it's not that far to the lows of a world-famous valley. Glencoe combines jaw-dropping scenery with a sometimes tragic history. The 'Valley of Weeping', situated on the main route north through the Highlands, has a melancholy, haunted feel. Perhaps that's due to the infamous massacre of 1692.

The region boasts a wonderful collection of mountain peaks, ridges, rushing rivers and waterfalls, which together create a magical landscape offering a diverse range of activities and plenty of space to roam free. The road climbs over the bleak expanse of Rannoch Moor before dropping between the steep, scree-strewn sides of the glen. Breathtaking mountains such as Buachaille Etive Mor and the Three Sisters loom on either side, with riverine scenery at the bottom.

The area is a paradise for walkers and climbers in all seasons, and skiers and snowboarders in the winter. Visitors can hire mountain bikes and hurtle downhill on purpose-built bike tracks, or you might fancy climbing, or simply walking the miles of mountain and forestry tracks. Or you could simply stand and stare at a landscape that never fails to astonish.

It's probable that Eilean Donan Castle appears on more shortbread tins than any other, and it's easy to understand why. Sitting on its own little island overlooking the Isle of Skye, at a point where three great sea lochs meet and surrounded by the majestic forested mountains of Kintail, Eilean Donan's setting is eye-popping.

Crossing the bridge to today's castle, the fourth version, you can see why Bishop Donan chose this tranquil spot in 634 AD to create a monastic cell. The first castle was established in the thirteenth century by Alexander II in an effort to help protect the area from Viking incursions. Over the centuries, it contracted and expanded for mysterious reasons until 1719, when it was involved in one of the lesser-known Jacobite uprisings. Blown apart following the quelling of that rebellion, Eilean Donan lay in silent ruin for the best part of two hundred years.

The castle that visitors enjoy today was reconstructed as a family home between 1912 and 1932, incorporating much of the ruins from the 1719 destruction. At this point the memorable bridge was added. Visitors can wander round most of the castle's internal rooms viewing period furniture, Jacobean artefacts, displays of weapons and fine art.

It's the largest and the best known of the Inner Hebrides, it was voted fourth best

Above: *Eilean Donan Castle, Loch Duich – named after Saint Donnán of Eigg, who was martyred in 617 AD*

island in the world by *National Geographic* magazine and it's one of Scotland's most popular destinations. It's the Isle of Skye.

Skye, renowned for its rugged beauty, wildlife, history and geology, is a paradise for hill-walkers and other outdoor activity practitioners. Its landscape has a distinctly Highland feel, with its lochs, heather-topped moors and lofty peaks, yet you're always aware you're on a small island.

Walkers are usually keen to tackle the heights of the Cuillin mountain range. It is Cuillin that is literally Skye's most outstanding feature and the peaks, visible from all over the island, make up one of the most glorious sights Scotland has to offer. Other geological marvels include the astounding sea cliff of Kilt Rock and the extraordinary landslip formation of the Quiraing.

The island provides a home for wildlife ranging from red deer and wildcats to pine martens and mountain hares. Cruises offer the chance to spot seals, dolphins, otters, golden eagles and sea eagles. Back on dry land, the capital, Portree, has a pastel cottage-lined harbour overlooked by a hill known as The Lump.

The West Mainland of Orkney contains a collection of Neolithic relics that are unsurpassed in Europe. The Heart of Neolithic Orkney, a UNESCO World Heritage Site, includes the ancient Ring of Brodgar, the Stones of Stenness, the Maeshowe tomb and Skara Brae, along with other excavated and unexcavated sites.

The stone circles of Brodgar and Stenness, dating back to 3100 and 2500 BC respectively, are perfect representations of Orkney's ancient heritage. Not all the original stones still stand, but it is difficult to comprehend the effort expended in the creation of these vast rings.

Maeshowe is the grandest chambered tomb on Orkney. Viking raiders left their mark on Maeshowe in the twelfth century, and you can still see their runic graffiti. The original purpose of the structures is unknown, but it's thought they could have been part of a ceremonial area. Skara Brae is an impressive complex of Neolithic homes constructed around 3000 BC. Concealed beneath sand dunes until 1850, the dwellings provide a striking insight into life in Orkney at this time.

And on Orkney our whirlwind tour of some of Scotland's most precious treasures is complete. Haste ye back.

Far Left: Ring of Brodgar, West Mainland, Orkney – Neolithic stone circle whose exact age remains uncertain

Fascinating Scotland

Scotland, with a land area of 78,387 square kilometres (30,265 square miles), is roughly the same size as the US state of Maine and the Japanese island of Hokkaido.

The mythical unicorn is Scotland's official animal. A 'unicorn's horn' at Dunvegan Castle, the home of the Clan MacLeod on the Isle of Skye, was found upon investigation to belong to an eland (a large African antelope).

What do haggis, kilts, bagpipes, whisky and tartan have in common? The answer is *not* that they all come from Scotland; in fact quite the opposite. The ancient Greeks ate haggis; kilts originated in Ireland; bagpipes came from the Middle East; whisky was first distilled in either China or Ireland, depending on whom you believe; and peoples in central Europe wore tartan between 400 and 100 BC.

The world's shortest scheduled flight – a hop of one and a half miles from Westray to Papa Westray in the Orkney Islands – takes a mere one minute and fourteen seconds.

On 21 June 1919, while negotiations took place over their fate, seventy-two ships of the German fleet were interned in the Royal Navy's base at Scapa Flow in the Orkney Islands. The

fleet's commander, Admiral Ludwig von Reuter, fearing his ships would be divided among the allied powers, ordered them to be scuttled. Despite the intervention of guard ships, fifty-two vessels sank.

The oldest continuously operating military airbase in the world is RAF Leuchars in Fife. It was established in 1908.

The Hamilton Mausoleum, built to accommodate the remains of the Dukes of Hamilton in the South Lanarkshire town of the same name, has the longest-lasting echo of any man-made structure. Slamming the entrance doors produces an echo of fifteen seconds. The building's extraordinary acoustic properties mean two people can conduct a whispered conversation at opposite ends of one of the mausoleum's curved walls.

The Bank of Scotland, founded in 1695, was the first bank in Europe to print its own notes. It is the second oldest surviving bank in the UK after the Bank of England.

The motto Nemo me impune lacessit, which appears on the royal coat of arms of the Kingdom of Scotland, translates as 'No one can harm me unpunished', or, in Scots, 'Wha daur meddle wi me?'

Britain's oldest building is the stone-built Neolithic settlement of Skara Brae on Orkney. It was occupied between 3180 BCE and 2500 BCE but was only rediscovered in 1850, when stormy weather ripped away the earth of a knoll known to local people as Skerrabra.

Tourists often curse midges, the tiny flying and biting insects that plague parts of Scotland during the summer. Queen Victoria is said to have smoked cigarettes as a way of keeping midges at bay. Want to go where the midges aren't? Consult the invaluable Midge Forecast at midgeforecast.co.uk.

In 1945 the Kennedy family thanked President Dwight D Eisenhower on behalf of the Scottish people for America's support during World War II by offering him the lifetime tenancy of a guest flat on the top floor of Culzean Castle in Ayrshire. Ike and family members stayed there several times, and he also lent the flat to friends.

Around five million people of Scottish ancestry live in the United States and Canada – as many as the current population of Scotland.

The inventor William Symington tested the world's first steamboat on Dalswinton Loch, north of Dumfries, on 14 October 1788. Some accounts stated that the poet Robert Burns, a near neighbour, was on board the boat as it chugged along at five miles an hour.

The thistle was adopted as the emblem of Scotland in the reign of Alexander III (1249-1286). Popular legend states that a Norse raiding party intent on attacking Largs took off their footwear so as not to be heard. One raider stood on a prickly thistle and let out a yelp that alerted the Scots, who drove off the enemy. The thistle became a royal symbol of Scotland when it was featured on coins issued by James III in 1470.

Aberdeen removals, haulage and storage firm The Shore Porters Society is the oldest transport company in the world – it was founded in 1498, a mere six years after Columbus first set foot in America.

Alexander Selkirk – also known as Selcraig – was a Scottish sailor who in the early eighteenth century spent four years marooned on an uninhabited island

Far Left: *Queen Victoria with her servant and favourite John Brown – was she a smoker?*

Above: *Whisky – where was it first distilled?*

in the South Pacific archipelago of Juan Fernández. He built huts, made clothes from goatskin and, when his musket ammunition ran out, chased prey on foot in order to eat. The writer Daniel Defoe heard Selkirk's story, was intrigued and based the hero of his novel *Robinson Crusoe* on him.

Common Ridings, held in Border towns each summer, commemorate the medieval times when horse riders would protect towns' boundaries against raiders. Nowadays, costumed riders astride hundreds of horses recall those times.

The town of Selkirk claims it has one of Europe's largest mounted cavalcades.

Around 650,000 people in Scotland – thirteen per cent of the population – have red hair. This compares with a worldwide figure of between one and two per cent.

The saltire, or Saint Andrew's cross, features on the Scottish flag as a diagonal white cross on a blue background. Saint Andrew, Scotland's patron saint, is said to have been martyred on an x-shaped cross. He and his brother

Peter, both fishermen, are said to have been called by Jesus to become 'fishers of men'.

A tenth century Latin Gospel Book, *The Book of Deer* (*Leabhar Dhèir*), contains the earliest known example of written Gaelic. The book was probably written at the first Abbey of Deer in Buchan, north of Aberdeen.

The second-largest granite building in the world can be found in Aberdeen, which is justly called the Granite City. Only the historical residence of the King of Spain, El Escorial in San Lorenzo, Spain is bigger than Marischal College. The building is nowadays the headquarters of Aberdeen City Council, but it was formerly the seat of the city's university.

James Braidwood, at the early age of 24, became the founder of the first municipal fire service in the world when he formed Edinburgh's brigade in 1824. He communicated with his firefighters via a boatswain's pipe.

The Big Grey Man of Ben MacDhui is the name given to a creature or presence said to haunt the Cairngorm Mountains. It is, according to various witnesses, either a very tall figure covered with short hair or an invisible but terrifying presence.

Scotland's national poet, Robert Burns, was brought up in poverty, and hard manual labour on farms in his childhood left him with a stoop and poor physical condition. A stint of training to be a flax dresser in Irvine came to an end when the flax shop burnt to the ground.

It is possible to throw a stone from the North Sea to the Atlantic Ocean on the thirty-three metre-wide Mavis Grind, an isthmus that connects Shetland Mainland to the Northmavine peninsula.

No wonder Tiree, the most westerly island in the Inner Hebrides, is a popular spot for windsurfing. According to the weather statistics, it's the windiest place in the British Isles, with the highest average gusts of over 160 kilometres an hour (100 mph).

The hallways of the Regency houses of Edinburgh's New Town – mostly built between 1765 and 1850 – were designed wide enough to allow the occupants of sedan chairs to be delivered safe, sound and dry into their abodes.

Glasgow has more public parks than any other city in Britain. Its 70-plus green spaces give rise to Glasgow's affectionate nickname Dear Green Place.

It's often said that according to the results of a census carried out in 1909, the Scots were the tallest race in Europe. But the Great War is reputed to have had a drastic effect on their stature: by the 1930s, the average height of men in Scotland had fallen by nine inches.

It's easy to miss the River Morar. It's only five hundred metres long, and is thus Scotland's shortest river.

When it opened in 1903, Hampden Park in Glasgow was the biggest stadium in the world. The record stood until 1950. On 17 April 1937, when Scotland played England, 149,547 spectators squeezed into Hampden's confines. That was the official attendance, at any rate; twenty thousand further fans are thought to have entered without tickets.

Local legend has it that Pontius Pilate was born in the shade of the famous ancient yew tree of Fortingall. It's impossible to verify that claim, but it is certain that the tree is very, very old – between two thousand and five thousand years.

The Atholl Highlanders infantry regiment was established as the Duke of Atholl's bodyguard in 1839. It is still employed by the current Duke and is the only legal private army in Europe.

The eighth Laird of Merchistoun, John Napier, was the first to publish the method of logarithms in his 1614 book *Description of the Wonderful Rule of Logarithms*, and thus puzzle many generations of schoolchildren. A physicist, astronomer and astrologer as well as a mathematician, Napier also invented the Napier's Bones abacus.

Britain's smallest cathedral can be found in the town of Millport on the Isle of Cumbrae. Visitors often find the Cathedral of the Isles, which dates from 1851, hard to locate, nestling as it does among trees behind the town.

The ten most common surnames in Scotland are Smith, Brown, Wilson, Thomson, Robertson, Campbell, Stewart, Anderson, MacDonald and Scott.

The highest temperature ever recorded in Scotland was a relatively cool 32.9 degrees Celsius. The heatwave occurred on 9 August 2003 at Greycrook in the Borders.

Scotland lost more soldiers per head of population than any other country in World War I. It is thought around 100,000 Scots perished in the Great War.

Glasgow's Mitchell Library, established in 1877 thanks to a bequest from a tobacco manufacturer, is the largest public reference library in Europe.

The Chapel of St Oran, next to Iona Abbey in the Hebrides, was named after Odhráin, a follower of St Columba. The graveyard, which has been in use since the saint's time, is reputed to be the burial ground of forty-eight Dalriadan and Scottish kings (including Macbeth), eight monarchs of Norway and four from Ireland.

The church in the former fishing village of St Monans in Fife sits on the very edge of the North Sea. In olden times, a bell hanging from a tree in the kirkyard was silenced during the herring

FASCINATING SCOTLAND

fishing season, as local superstition held that its loud tolling would frighten the fish away.

Mary Stuart, otherwise known as Mary, Queen of Scots, was so fond of white that she insisted on wearing that colour for her wedding to the Dauphin of France, Francis, in 1558. Her fashion sense caused something of a stir, for white was regarded as the colour of mourning in sixteenth century France.

Sixty-three per cent of Scots have pure blue eyes, but that figure is surpassed in Scandinavian and Baltic countries – and in Ireland, where sixty-six per cent of the population are blue-eyed.

A widespread disease that sounds remarkably similar to today's bird flu was described in Scotland in the fourteenth century.

Scotland has the highest waterfall in Britain. Eas a' Chual Aluinn, in Sutherland, has a sheer drop of two hundred metres (656 feet). When in full flow it's over three times higher than Niagara Falls. The name is a corruption of the Gaelic for 'waterfall of the beautiful tresses'.

The Act of Union of 1707 largely ended the argument over whether Berwick-upon-Tweed belonged to Scotland or England. Over the course of four hundred years up to 1482, the town changed hands more than a dozen times. It's now officially in England – although Berwick's football team plays in the Scottish Football League.

The surface of Loch Ness is 15.8 metres (fifty-two feet) above sea level. The loch contains more fresh water than all the lakes of England and Wales combined.

And finally ... the worst 'Scottish' accent ever recorded on film – beating Canadian James Doohan's bizarre efforts as Scottie in *Star Trek* and Mel Gibson's strangulated brogue in *Braveheart* – was officially Christopher Lambert's mysterious vocal performance in *Highlander*. Described as sounding like the utterances of a drunken Norwegian, the accent gathered forty-two per cent of votes in a 2008 poll.

ALSO AVAILABLE IN THE LITTLE BOOK SERIES

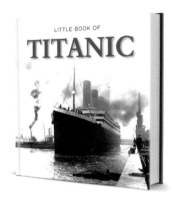

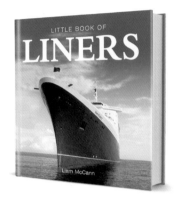

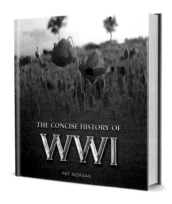

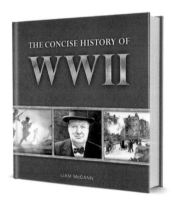

ALSO AVAILABLE IN THE LITTLE BOOK SERIES

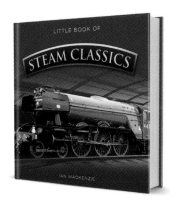

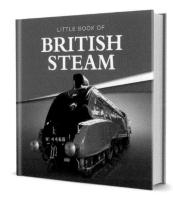

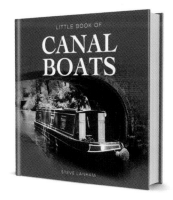

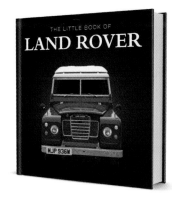

The pictures in this book were provided courtesy of the following:

WIKIMEDIA COMMONS

Design & Artwork: SCOTT GIARNESE

Published by: DEMAND MEDIA LIMITED & G2 ENTERTAINMENT LIMITED

Publishers: JASON FENWICK & JULES GAMMOND

Written by: PAT MORGAN